That day, standing in front of Janna's mirror, I wished that someday I could have something that Janna didn't have—something all my own, that would make me interesting and important in everyone's eyes.

They say you should never wish for something, because you might get it. That's very true.

A month after my fourteenth birthday, I did get something Janna didn't have. And it did make me very interesting and important to a lot of people, like my family and a bunch of doctors and nurses.

What I got was cancer of the blood. It's called leukemia.

BEBE FAAS RICE is the author of many books for young adults. She lives in Falls Church, Virginia.

Day by Day

My Sister, My Sorrow
Bebe Faas Rice

LAUREL-LEAF BOOKS

Published by
Dell Publishing
a division of
Bantam Doubleday Dell Publishing Group, Inc.
666 Fifth Avenue
New York, New York 10103

The trademark Laurel-Leaf Library® is registered in the U.S. Patent and Trademark Office.

The trademark Dell® is registered in the U.S. Patent and Trademark Office.

ISBN: 0-440-21296-0

RL:6.0

Printed in the United States of America

June 1992

10 9 8 7 6 5 4 3 2 1

OPM

To my husband, whose Star Quality lights up my life

1

On my fourteenth birthday, Uncle Ed Farrell said the worst possible thing.

"That Janna," he said, "has what's called Star Quality."

My name is Beth. Uncle Ed was not talking about me. Janna, the one with the Star Quality, is my sister. My beautiful, perfect sister. The rose without a thorn. The diamond without a flaw.

Janna is three years older than I am and has been the apple of everyone's eye for as long as I can remember. Take this birthday party, for example. Here were all the relatives sitting around our big dining room table, eating ice cream and cake. I was the center of attention for a change. The happy birthday song had been sung and I'd blown out all the candles with one puff. Toasts had been made to my glorious future. Aunt Flo had even remarked on how closely I was beginning to resemble Grandmother Manning, Dad's mother, which really made me feel good because Gran was supposed to have been quite a looker in her time.

So there I was, basking happily in the limelight. Then, wham! Uncle Ed had to horn in with that thing about Janna.

The terrible thing is, Janna *does* have Star Quality. I've always known it, but up until that moment I couldn't quite put a name to it.

Uncle Ed went on to say that he'd just seen the musical *Evita* at the Bonnie Buffet Dinner Theater, and in it the Eva Perón character, realizing she is destined for Argentinian fame and fortune, belts out this song about how she's on her way up, and everyone better stand back because she's got —you guessed it—Star Quality.

"When I heard that term, Star Quality," he said, "I realized that's what Janna has—that something special that sets her apart from everybody else."

I saw Mom's mouth tighten at that. She always says that Uncle Ed needs sensitivity training, and she's very aware of the fact that I feel I'm only Janna's lackluster, no-talent nothing of a kid sister. She worries about it. A lot.

That's why she'd planned this family party for me. She'd said, "Please, Beth, let us give you one last big family birthday party. Next year I expect

Okay, so maybe I lied about dinner.

The truth is, I had broiled flounder. With lima beans, no less.

But a girl can dream, can't she? And let's face it, this bogus food diary doesn't exactly make for juicy reading.

Other thirteen-year-olds write in their diaries about guys, or parties, or school. Or maybe even their secret fantasies.

I write about broiled flounder.

Correct me if I'm wrong here, but I seem to be missing something.

Like a life.

Oops. I'm doing it again. Negative thinking. Whenever I do that, Dr. Patterson says I'm supposed to take a deep, cleansing breath and think about something positive. And not something positive like warm chocolate chip cookies either.

Dr. Patterson's my psychiatrist here. She's very big on cleansing breaths. As far as I'm concerned, air is air, but who am I to argue? She's the one who went to shrink school.

This journal is Dr. Patterson's idea too. Keeping track of what I eat is supposed to help me change my attitude toward food. But when I write *cauliflower*, I think *chocolate*. I don't exactly see how that's helping my attitude problem.

I'm also supposed to be baring my soul in this diary. You know, putting my feelings down on paper, in between the skim milk and the tuna fish and the endless parade of good-for-you vegetables. Dr. P. says writing down my emotions will help me feel better about myself.

Fine, Dr. Patterson. Here's what I'm feeling. *I hate it here. I hate it here. I hate it here.*

I've been here at Hopeless House two whole days and it's very clear to me that a terrible mistake has been made. I do not belong here. There are sick people in this place. Very sick people. I am not sick. I am hungry.

When I say "Hopeless House" in front of Dr. P., she just shakes her head. "It's called *Hope* House for a very good reason, Zibby," she said during my therapy session this morning. "A lot of the kids staying here are very sick. Some will be chronically ill for their whole lives. A few may even die. You're lucky because you can get better, if you let us help you."

"But I don't need to be here," I argued. And it's true. I've got things under control. Really. And deep breaths and diaries are not going to change the way I live my life.

I'll tell you what would change my life. A couple of pounds of chocolate and a one-way ticket out of this place.

SOMEONE, GET ME OUT OF HERE!

Sorry, Dr. P. I have now written down my feelings, and I do not—repeat, DO NOT—feel better about myself. So much for your diary theory.

She told me I could be in here weeks. A couple months, even. I told her no way.

I've escaped from some pretty tough places. Pep rallies. Family reunions. Orthodontist appointments. Even after-school detention.

Mark my words. I'm busting out of here too.

Gotta go now. Here come the calorie cops. (Otherwise known as nurses.) It's time for our evening snack.

It's a pretty safe bet they won't be serving Snickers Bars.

you'll want one of those loud, awful high school things."

What she really meant, though, was that she wanted to do something that would make me feel special and in the spotlight, and who can make you feel more special than a collection of aunts and uncles? And Irish ones at that.

I knew perfectly well that was what Mom was trying to do. In the first place, she's as transparent as glass. In the second, I found the book she'd been reading. It was titled *Sibling Rivalry and the Adolescent.*

And here was Uncle Ed, raining on my parade.

Mom opened her mouth to say something, but Janna beat her to it.

"But Uncle Ed," she protested. "We Mannings *all* have Star Quality, although sometimes Beth acts more like Halley's Comet, at least in the morning when she's rushing out of the house."

Everyone laughed at that and the party continued.

Which brings me to the second terrible thing about Janna. She is as good as she is beautiful.

It sounds like someone in a fairy tale, doesn't it? You know, the lovely princess who was as good as she was beautiful? Well, corny as it sounds, it still happens in real life, although in books nowadays the gorgeous ones usually turn out to be spoiled and selfish.

When I was little, I used to read a lot of fairy tales. I liked all those beautiful and good princesses because they reminded me of my wonderful big sister.

I really loved Janna in those days. It was a kind of idol worship on my part, and Janna was always everything a big sister should be. She still is. That's why it's hard for me to understand my feelings about her now. Whenever she does something especially nice for me, I get this awful, guilty feeling because I don't feel the same about her as I did before—because I know I'm not as nice to her as she is to me.

Anyway, back in the days when I was reading all those fairy tales, I knew perfectly well I was small and skinny and not at all beautiful like Janna, but it didn't bother me. I was simply proud and happy to be her sister. None of my other friends had a sister as nice as mine.

Janna used to take me everywhere—to the swimming pool and on picnics. She taught me a lot of things, too, like how to swim and draw and play tennis. She was always there for me when I needed her.

And then, in the summer after seventh grade, I turned against her.

Every Easter on television, they replay that old Charlton Heston version of *Ben-Hur*. You've probably seen it as many times as I have. If you'll recall, Ben-Hur has a childhood friend named Messala. They were the closest of friends until something happens and Messala turns against Ben-Hur. Not only turns against him, but becomes a terrible, deadly enemy.

I don't like to watch that movie anymore because I feel just like Messala—mean and rotten to the core. But he couldn't help what he was and neither can I.

It's funny, isn't it, how you can look back and pinpoint exactly where something happened that changed your life forever. Someone can say something or do something and you're never quite the same afterward.

Well, that summer (was it only a year and a half ago? It seems much longer) Mom and Dad gave Janna permission to redecorate her bedroom. I was sulky and put out about it because I wanted to do mine, too, but Mom only said, "No, Beth. When you're Janna's age you may redecorate, but not until then."

To be fair to myself, I have to say that I'd been moody and temperamental for a couple of months before all this happened. Our seventh grade health and hygiene teacher had tried to prepare us for what my friends and I were starting to go through. She'd explained that we would all be experiencing bodily changes that would also affect our emotions, but that, in time, things would straighten themselves out. Meanwhile, she said, we should try to be sensible and mature and not give in to our moods and emotions when we knew we were being unreasonable.

Easier said than done. I doubted that Ms. Snyder had ever felt as weepy and nasty as I did sometimes. If this is growing up, I thought, I've changed my mind. I'm not going to do it after all.

I remember I was feeling crabby the day Janna finished redoing her bedroom. I'd mysteriously developed a couple of big red zits on my chin and my hair was lank and yucky, even though I'd just washed it the day before. I felt like a real mess.

"Ta da!" sang out Janna from the doorway to her room.

She was wearing a white sundress. Her thick, shining black hair was pulled back with an Alice band. Her skin, naturally, was perfect—pale and creamy with a flush of rose along the cheekbones. Her blue eyes sparkled.

I thought of that fairy tale, *Snow White*. Her mother, the queen, had wished for a daughter with hair black as ebony, skin white as snow, and rosy lips. And here she was, in the living flesh, reincarnated as Janna Manning.

All she needs is a Prince Charming, but I'm sure one is on the way, I thought. Everything good always happens to *her*!

It was a petty, niggly little thought, and I remember feeling surprised at myself. Of course Janna deserved good things happening to her! Didn't she?

Aloud I said, "You mean I get to see your room at long last?"

"That's right," said Janna. "I wanted to wait until everything was absolutely perfect before I put it on view."

She stepped back and made an elaborate gesture, like a magician opening a trunk. "But first, please observe my door."

Our upstairs hallway is long and narrow, flanked by five doorways opening into four bedrooms and a bath. The doors were painted a cream white. All except one. Janna's door. It was a pale, pale mauve. She'd been busy with a paint can and brushes for days and the door was her final touch.

Then I saw the doorknob. An ordinary brass one had been on the door earlier that morning, but now there was a new one.

"Do you like it, Beth? I found it at a flea market. Don't you think it's absolutely perfect?"

Yes, it was perfect. Perfect for a princess or a movie star or a great stage actress.

It was one of those antique cut crystal doorknobs you see in fine old homes, only this one was amethyst in color—a glittering amethyst doorknob on a pale mauve door. Only Janna could have come up with something like that—Janna, the Star.

I told her how nice it looked, trying to sound sincere and unselfish, and she showed me into her room.

That's when it hit me—the pang of envy so powerful I felt as if I'd been kicked in the stomach. The room looked like something out of one of those decorator home magazines.

The walls were painted the palest shade of a mauvey lavender, and she'd papered the wall behind her bed in a Victorian print of trailing lavender roses on a cream background. She and Mom had made curtains out of matching fabric for her large double windows.

Two new boudoir chairs in a mauve chintz stood before the window with a table, covered in the same fabric as the curtains, between them.

She'd done the bed in vintage white linens that she said she'd found in flea markets, then bleached, starched, and ironed. The bed was draped with a crisp white spread and was piled high with pillows in all shapes and sizes, encased in white linen and edged with lace.

I thought about my bed with its dirty old stuffed animals and felt sick.

"But this," she said, pulling me over to the corner, "is the pièce de résistance. Mom and Dad gave it to me as a sort of reward for doing most of the labor on the room myself. I think it's called a *cheval glass*."

She was talking about a full-length oval mirror that was attached to a standing frame. You could tilt it back and forth. She tilted it so the two of us, standing together, were framed in it, like in an old-fashioned photograph.

There we were—Snow White and Dopey, Beauty and the Beast, Miss America and The Swamp Thing.

I was almost as tall as she was at that point, which made the contrast between us even worse. We didn't look like Big Sister Janna and her faithful little shadow anymore. That part of our lives, I realized with a start, was over. My thirteenth birthday was coming up in a couple of months and I'd be a teenager, just like Janna. No, not just like Janna. Wouldn't I give anything for *that*!

Seeing the two of us side by side in the mirror was like being given a sudden glimpse of the future. I'd always had some childish idea that being and looking like Janna was merely a matter of growing older. I realized that day that I could never be like Janna. We were different. Completely, totally different.

At the time I actually remember Janna saying something about how much we looked alike, that our eyes were exactly the same shade of blue. But

I chalked it up as another instance of wonderful Janna being kind to her pitiful little sister.

She'll always be the pretty one, the pretty, clever, talented one that people notice and admire, I thought despairingly. And I'll always be the plain, nothing one, slopping along behind her. And I bet, I thought, relishing the pain the way you do when you bite on a sore tooth, and I just bet when we're older, strangers will ask, "Oh, are you two sisters? I never would have guessed!" And of course, I thought darkly, I'll know what they mean.

I'd never been an envious, jealous person, but I guess anyone can be, given the right set of circumstances. I should know. It happened to me.

Jealousy is a terrible thing. They call it "the green-eyed monster" but that doesn't even half begin to describe it. It's like having an ugly devil inside you that eats away at you—chew! chew! chew!—all the time.

So that was to be my future, an ugly devil chewing away on me inside while on the outside I tried to act like a normal person. Obviously I didn't fool my family. I could see the hurt in Janna's eyes sometimes when I'd acted sharp and snippy with her. And here was Mom, buying books like *Sibling Rivalry and the Adolescent* and trying to build up my self-image.

That day, standing in front of Janna's mirror, I

wished that someday I could have something that Janna didn't have—something all my own, that would make me interesting and important in everyone's eyes.

They say you should never wish for something, because you might get it. That's very true.

A month after my fourteenth birthday, I did get something Janna didn't have. And it did make me very interesting and important to a lot of people, like my family and a bunch of doctors and nurses.

What I got was cancer of the blood. It's called leukemia.

2

There are several kinds of leukemia. The kind I developed was acute lymphocytic leukemia, the most common childhood cancer.

My first reaction was, *There must be some mistake! This can't be happening to me!*

It wasn't a mistake. It was happening.

My second was, *Why me?*

There isn't any answer to that one, but it was the question that bothered me the most. If it hadn't been for my friends at Hope House . . . well, I'll tell you about them later.

Leukemia is one of those diseases that creep up on you suddenly and catch you by surprise.

It started with me losing weight and feeling tired all the time. I've never been heavy, so even a five-pound weight loss shows up right away. I remember even at my fourteenth birthday noticing how roomy the waist of my red pleated skirt had become.

Naturally my mother, the vigilante, thought I had one of those eating disorders a lot of girls get these days and started snooping around to see if I was taking laxatives or deliberately barfing up my meals.

I wasn't, but I was running a constant low-grade fever and getting bruises for no good reason. I may be a klutz, but I *do* know when and where I've bumped myself hard enough to bring on one of those awful-looking things. Then my gums started to bleed. My toothbrush in the morning looked like an accessory to a suicide attempt. That's when Mom took me to Dr. Cohen, our family doctor.

Dr. Cohen is gentle, patient, and thorough and says, "Hmmm" and "Ah-huh" a lot.

He checked me over, hmmming and ah-huhing, then sent me off to the lab for blood work.

He didn't just telephone with the results, but called Mom and me into his office.

"I want Beth to have a further consultation with a colleague of mine. Tomorrow morning, if that's convenient with you," he told us. "His name is Dr. Lindberg, and he's a specialist working out of St. Stephen's Hospital in Somerset."

Somerset, Indiana, is a fairly good-sized city about thirty miles from us. St. Stephen's Hospital is quite well known. It's a large, well-equipped hospital, very modern, very well staffed. A little prickle of fear ran over the hairs on my forearms. What kind of specialist? And why Somerset?

Mom echoed my thoughts. "What are you talking about, Doctor? *A specialist?* Doesn't Beth simply need a good tonic or vitamin shots or something?"

Dr. Cohen shifted uneasily in his chair. "I don't want to worry you, Mrs. Manning, but Beth's blood doesn't look quite right. Dr. Lindberg is an oncologist, and I'd like him to do some further tests."

"Further tests?" Mom sounded bewildered. "And what, exactly, is an oncologist?"

I could tell Dr. Cohen was stalling for time because he fiddled with his eyeglasses for a moment —removing them, polishing them with his handkerchief, and then putting them back on. Finally he said, "An oncologist is a doctor who specializes in diagnosing and treating cancer. Dr. Lindberg's further specialty is pediatric leukemia."

Pediatric leukemia. I could almost see the words written in the air between us in flowing script.

Dr. Cohen went on to say that the blood test he'd given me did not establish a firm diagnosis of leukemia, but pointed toward its possibility. He laid it all out for us, squarely and honestly, yet he tried to be as hopeful and optimistic as he could.

I'll never forget that night, with Mom out in the kitchen, sobbing as she scraped the carrots for dinner. Artists and sculptors usually depict Grief as a heavily veiled figure leaning on a tombstone, but they're wrong. What Grief really is, is a middle-aged woman with a carrot parer in one hand, laying her head down on the sink.

As for my dad—well, he didn't know what to say. He has this funny vein in his forehead that stands out when he's upset about something. It was standing out that night. All he could do was hug me occasionally and say to my mom, "Now, now, Annie. We aren't sure yet, are we? Let's just wait until we see what the doctor says tomorrow before we jump to any conclusions. Please, Annie. I can't bear to see you cry like this."

And Janna . . . I remember looking over at her and thinking, *Why me? Why not her?* And then feeling a guilt so terrible and shaming that I was afraid I'd be hit by a thunderbolt from heaven.

Janna kept saying that it couldn't possibly be true—that there must have been a mistake in the laboratory with the blood work, and that tomorrow we'd find out that everything was fine, just fine . . .

* * *

But it wasn't fine. Dr. Lindberg did a bone marrow test on me and it turned out that yes, I did have acute lymphocytic leukemia.

Taking the sample of my bone marrow wasn't at all as bad as it sounds. It was done right in the office with a local anesthetic. I've had to have a lot of them since then in the course of monitoring my disease.

My disease. My leukemia.

I was glad I'd done all my crying the night before, because now I needed a clear head to find out what could be done to make me better.

I don't mean to make myself sound spunky and courageous. I wasn't, not in the least. Part of it was just whistling in the dark, and part of it was Mom sitting there looking ragged. And part of it was because there was nothing else I *could* do. Then there was Dr. Lindberg. He has a real buckuppo way of speaking that makes you want to go out there and give it your best.

"You must remember, Beth," he said, "that this is only a diagnosis, not a death sentence. The treatment of childhood leukemia is one of the great success stories of cancer therapy."

He leaned forward, his blue eyes eager and intense.

"Tremendous progress has been made in the past few years in the treatment of cancer. We have new anticancer drugs and improved methods of radiation therapy now. We're seeing long-term remissions and actual cures!"

"So what do we do next?" I asked.

"I'm going to put you in St. Stephen's immediately and start you on chemotherapy and radiation therapy," Dr. Lindberg replied. "Our aim is to get you into a state of complete remission as quickly as possible."

Up until then Mom had been pretty quiet. At least for her. Her eyes were still puffy from last night, and when she did say something, her voice was a little too loud and falsely cheery.

"You mean . . . *cured*?" she asked hopefully.

The doctor shook his head.

"I wish it were that simple, Mrs. Manning," he said, "but that's not how it works. You see, a state of complete remission means that your laboratory tests show that you have none of the signs of leukemia, and that you can live a normal, healthy life. However—"

"However?" echoed my mother.

"However, there is always a chance of relapse," he said, "so we will have to keep Beth on maintenance therapy for several years and watch her closely."

"And then what?" I asked.

"Relapse after five years of complete remission is rare," said Dr. Lindberg. "Patients whose remission lasts that long may be considered cured, and that's what we're shooting for with you."

"And it's going to happen. I just know it," said Mom.

"I'd like to check Beth into St. Stephen's tomorrow afternoon, Mrs. Manning," said the doctor. "Can you have her ready?"

"Of course. And can you tell me, Doctor, how long we might expect her to remain there?"

"Possibly six weeks or so."

"That long? Why?" Mom asked.

"We'll be using some pretty potent drugs on Beth and she will experience a number of side effects," he replied. "We'll want to keep a close eye on her. Then, when she's released from St. Stephen's, I'm going to recommend she stay at Hope House for an indefinite period."

"Hope House?"

"It's an infirmary for children and teenagers with serious illnesses," he explained. "It's connected with St. Stephen's. Dr. Lilly Gordon, who frequently works with me, is an oncologist on the staff there. I'd like to have her monitor Beth's blood and do frequent physical exams and evaluations on her for a while. And Dr. Graham, who heads Hope House, is a psychologist. It will be convenient for Beth to receive therapy while she's there."

"You mean I'll need a shrink?" I asked in dismay.

"Yes. It's automatically a part of the treatment we at St. Stephen's give cancer patients. You'll need to be able to sit down and talk to someone about what you're going through. Believe me, Beth, it helps."

Sitting there in Dr. Lindberg's office, I had my doubts about Hope House. Psychologists? Sick kids? It didn't exactly sound like my kind of place.

I got very little sleep the night before I checked into St. Stephen's.

I lay awake in my bed, nestled among my stuffed animals, listening to the comforting noises our house makes when it settles down for the night: a board creaking somewhere, the refrigerator making a *harumph* sound down in the kitchen, water running through the pipes in the walls as someone, probably Mom, completed her nightly ritual in the bathroom.

Even though I'd hated my bedroom when I had compared it to Janna's, I realized now how special it was to me. I felt safe here, surrounded by all the old familiar things I'd grown up with. And I realized it wouldn't be quite the same, somehow, when I returned to it.

I'll be like a soldier coming home from war, I thought. I will have experienced things my family and friends know nothing about. Maybe my room will seem foreign to me then.

I could only imagine what the following night would be like. I'd never been in a hospital before. Not even to have my tonsils removed. How like me, I thought, looking up at my moonlit ceiling, to skip all the easy stuff and go straight for a big, no-fooling-around disease like leukemia.

Leukemia. What an ugly, frightening word.

At the time, I didn't realize how something like leukemia makes people back away from you for one reason or other, and how weird your friends and family act when they're around you.

As it turned out, just about the only people I could talk to—really talk to—were the members of the staff at Hope House. And the kids. Especially Eliot.

3

I was feeling rather optimistic when I checked into the pediatric oncology ward at St. Stephen's Hospital. After all, Dr. Lindberg had said the treatment of childhood leukemia was one of the great success stories of cancer therapy, hadn't he? Maybe I'd just get my chemotherapy and then go into remission and stay that way forever.

Mom, Dad, and Janna accompanied me to my room. Mom was making a big fuss about whether or not my bedside bell worked and how on earth would I dial out on the telephone? I could hear her when I was in the bathroom changing into one of those awful hospital gowns that open all the way down the back. Mine was missing a couple of ties, so I had to clutch it behind me as I crawled into bed.

I had no roommate. The other bed was empty, its spread tucked neatly under the mattress.

"Aren't you lucky to have this room all to your-self?" Mom said. She smiled brightly, but the smile did not extend upward to her eyes. "She's probably been discharged because she's ever so much better now. Before long, you'll be home again, too, just you wait and see!"

I'm all for positive thinking, but Mom was beginning to sound like a hyperactive cheerleader. All she needed was a megaphone and pom-poms.

Her fake cheeriness made me uneasy. It reminded me of when I was little and she'd say, "This won't hurt a bit," as she dug a splinter out of my finger—and it would hurt like crazy. Or, "This is quite pleasant tasting, actually," as she gave me a spoonful of vile, disgusting medicine that turned my stomach.

As it turned out, there hadn't been a roommate. Mine had been a one-patient room for several months. So, instead of cheering me up, Mom's Pollyanna story of gladness and healing had the opposite effect. Why is she going on like this, I wondered. Does she know something I don't know? Something awful?

Dad fussed around the room, rearranging the chairs. He put one beside the window and then changed it back to its original position. "This is a nice hospital, Beth. It has the best of everything. You'll be well taken care of here."

His voice was husky, almost gruff, but he

reached over and gently smoothed my hair back from my forehead.

Ever since we found out I had leukemia, Dad, who is the strong silent type, had become even quieter. The vein in his forehead showed all the time now. As Mom got louder and cheerier, he grew more silent and withdrawn. I didn't know which parent was harder to take. I guess it was a tie.

Janna seemed fidgety, as if she didn't want to hang around. She kept fiddling with her hair and picking at her fingernails. She chipped the polish off one nail and started in on the next.

"I noticed your room at home needs a good cleaning, Beth," she said. "I'll dust and vacuum tomorrow, so it's ready for you when you leave Hope House."

She didn't look me in the eye when she said that. She knew perfectly well I'd be gone a long, long time.

Before my family left for home, Dr. Lindberg came to see them.

"I know I've already explained Beth's chemo-therapy to you, but I thought I'd stop by to see if there were any last-minute questions you might have."

I was beginning to like Dr. Lindberg more and more. I liked the way he listened very carefully to everything you said, and how he answered every question honestly.

"Nooo," Mom said, shaking her head thoughtfully. "I think you've covered just about everything."

"Okay," he said. "One last word of caution. We've discussed this earlier, but it bears repetition: Before Beth starts to feel better, she's going to suffer some rather unpleasant side effects of the chemotherapy—nausea, vomiting, hair loss. I do want you to remember, however, that if chemotherapy was not available, Beth's chance of remission would be very slight, indeed . . ."

Dr. Lindberg saying the side effects of my chemotherapy would be unpleasant was like Christopher Columbus telling his sailors that they might have a few little problems at sea. Sure I knew the going would be rough, but I couldn't have imagined how rough.

The chemo was given by series. Each series was called a *course.* I'd get a course of chemo, then a few days' rest, then another course. The chemo made me sick. I mean, *really* sick. I was so sick I would have had to get better in order to die.

They gave me pills for my nausea. They didn't work. They gave me Popsicles to settle my stomach. I soon learned to avoid the grape ones because they looked pretty ghastly in the basin when I threw them back up.

"Look on the bright side," Mom said on one of her daily visits. "Fifty years ago they didn't have all these marvelous drugs to treat your illness, so let's count our blessings."

I could have reminded her that fifty years ago I wasn't even alive, so I wouldn't have needed those new, marvelous drugs. But that would have been mean. Poor Mom. She tried so hard.

Leukemia literally means "white blood." It's not really a cancer of the blood itself, but of the organs that manufacture blood cells, mainly bone marrow and the lymph system. What happens is that the body starts cranking out a huge number of immature white blood cells that never mature or perform their proper functions. These defective cells then multiply like crazy. They fill the bone marrow, crowding out the healthy cells, and eventually spill out into the circulatory system. So the term "white blood" refers to the whitish or pale pink blood seen in patients with high amounts of circulating malignant white cells.

The main treatment of leukemia is chemotherapy. The theory behind it is to get enough of a certain type of drug into you to kill all the cells in the bone marrow—cancerous *and* normal. Since leukemia cells divide more slowly than normal ones, the healthy cells, growing faster, will repopulate the marrow. Then the continuing courses of chemo are designed to hit the regrowth cycles of leukemia cells and knock them out of commission.

The treatment takes about six weeks. First they give a drug to prevent kidney damage. Then comes three or four weeks of what they call "remission induction" where you're given chemotherapy, usually intravenously, followed by a couple of weeks of treatments to keep the leukemia from entering the cerebrospinal fluid. This is important because once cancerous cells get in there, they can't be reached by anticancer drugs. Sometimes they use radiation for this one, and sometimes they use injections.

After that, you have to stay on maintenance chemo for several years, but it isn't as bad as this first stuff, and can be done on an outpatient basis.

Chemotherapy really makes you tired, along with everything else. I almost lost track of time. And then one morning I woke up and found hair —lots of hair—on my pillow. Long, brown hair. My hair. I was losing my hair! I reached up and touched my head. A clump came off in my fingers.

Yes, I know, Dr. Lindberg had told me it would happen. And Mom tried to prepare me for it. She'd even sent away for a couple of those moviestar wigs that are advertised in the backs of magazines. Yet I had no idea it would happen like this.

That—bingo!—there it would be all over the pillow.

And that's when I went into the deep depression that scared my family and got the nurses all in a tizzy.

I read somewhere once that there are enough bald-headed women in the United States to fill a baseball stadium. When you think about it, that's a lot of bald-headed women. Yet thinking about it didn't make me feel one bit better. Those poor women were probably all as deep down depressed about it as I was.

What is it with women and hair? Why is thick, pretty hair so important to us and why do we fuss over it all the time?

I remember reading once about all the women who collaborated with the Nazis during World War II. Afterward, what was the worst punishment the townspeople could inflict on them? They shaved off all their hair, that's what. Those girls had to walk around bald-headed. That was their ultimate shame. I rest my case.

Janna came in one afternoon and cut the few remaining wisps short for me.

"There, that's neater," she said, putting her scissors back into her bag.

I looked at myself in a hand mirror.

"Now it's short and hideously thin instead of long and hideously thin," I moaned.

"You won't be like this forever, Beth," Janna said. There was a hint of reproof in her voice. "Your hair *will* grow back."

"But when? When?" I flung my arms out, palms up, like Moses praying for the Red Sea to part. "I could be bald for months, maybe. I am destroyed, Janna. Destroyed!"

"Oh, come on, Beth." Janna rose quickly and gathered up her belongings.

"Where are you going?" I asked.

"I've got to get to the library before it closes."

"You mean, I'm telling you I'm destroyed and you're leaving me here to suffer?"

Yes, I was being melodramatic and a pain in the neck, but I couldn't help it. I was between courses of chemo at the time and was feeling a little more energetic. But it was a grouchy, crabby energy, if you know what I mean.

"I'm sorry, Bethie, but I really do have to run. Your hair will grow back. What more can I say? You'll just have to be patient."

She slipped the strap of her bag over one shoulder and ran her fingers through her hair. Her long, thick, glossy hair.

The thing that needled me most was that she looked so *healthy*. The words, *Why me? Why not Janna?* whispered themselves in my ear. This was beginning to happen more and more often now, and the guilt that came with it only made things harder to bear.

"You do this all the time," I accused.

She looked over at me, surprised. Or was she just pretending to be surprised? "What? What do I do?"

"Rush off the minute I start to talk about something unpleasant."

Janna bent down and brushed a hasty kiss across my cheek. "I do not. We've spent all afternoon together. You're imagining things."

Then she quickly flitted out of the room like a butterfly doing windsprints.

"I am not imagining things," I said after she'd gone.

I turned my face to the window. As usual, I was feeling sorry for myself. *Why me?* I asked myself again. Have I done something terrible and this is my punishment? Is that it? Am I being punished for being jealous of Janna?

But if that was it, then *why me?* There were a couple of mean, jealous girls at school who were much worse than I was. Why didn't they get leukemia if it was supposed to be some sort of punishment? Compared to them, I was practically a saint.

I stared out the window. It was a drizzly, gray day, and little beads of rain were chasing each

other down the pane, mirroring the tears making
their way down my cheeks.

I didn't turn around, even when I heard someone enter the room.

"Ahem," said a male voice. It wasn't a throat-
clearing sound. It was the distinct word, "ahem,"
said comically like an amateur actor in a melo-
drama.

And that's how Eliot came into my life.

4

"Ahem," he said again.

I shifted my body to see who it was.

It was a pirate. At least, that was my first confused impression. A pirate on crutches with a lime green kerchief tied buccaneer style around his head. He was wearing faded cut-off jeans and a T-shirt with the picture of a large blue whale riding a tiny bicycle. SAVE THE TRAILS was written beneath the bicycle.

"Hi," he said.

He smiled a broad, friendly smile that spread across his cheeks and made his ears move a little. That's when I noticed he had no hair under the kerchief.

His kerchief must be concealing hair loss, I thought. Well, it made sense. This was an oncology ward. Here was another cancer patient, come to welcome me to the club.

He was about a year older than me, I guessed. He had blue eyes, set wide apart, and a jawline like that movie actor Rob Lowe has—you know, kind of square and well-boned looking. In my previous life, I would have considered him an absolute doll and would have sat up and tried to look cute and fun, but everything was different now. I didn't care how good looking he was, or whether he found me attractive or not. To heck with him. I only wanted to be left alone in my misery.

"My name's Eliot Randall," he said.

"Congratulations."

"Wrong answer. You're supposed to say, 'How do you do,' and tell me your name."

"Why? You probably know it already. I'll bet the nurses told you to come in here and cheer me up."

"No. Actually, they warned me against it. They practically begged me not to. They said, 'Stay away from that awful Beth Manning. She's mean as a snake!' "

I had to smile in spite of myself. "See?" I said. "You knew my name."

He leaned forward and squinted at me. "Is that a smile? And that hole in your cheek—is it a dimple or has someone been excavating your jaw?"

"Ha, ha, very funny. For your information, it's a dimple."

I waited a moment. "So why did you come in

here if they told you what a pain in the neck I am?"

"Because I'm a bold, dashing sort of fellow, in case you haven't noticed. I like a challenge."

I couldn't think of a reply to that one, so I gestured to the bedside chair. "Well, since you've made such an effort, would you like to sit down? I mean, unless you have something else to do."

Eliot eased himself into the bedside chair and placed his crutches carefully on the floor beside him.

"I thought you'd never ask, my dear. And no, I do not have something to do. I've watched enough soap operas and game shows to last me the rest of my life."

"What kind of cancer do you have?" I asked. "Is it in your leg?"

"Yes," he said. "Bone cancer. Mine's the kind known as *Ewing's sarcoma*."

"Is it bad? Does it hurt?"

Eliot stretched out his leg and rubbed it absently.

"Well, it's more a feeling of weakness than anything. They've already given me my courses of radiation and chemotherapy."

He pointed to his head. "That's how come I look like the original bald-headed eagle. But right now I'm in pretty good shape."

He looked over at me sympathetically. "Listen,

Beth, I know how sick and discouraged you must be feeling. I've been there myself and know how it feels. But hang tight. The nurses tell me you only have a couple more weeks to go before your induction therapy is over."

What a nice guy, I thought. The nurses must have told him how depressed I was and he came here just to cheer me up. And on his bum leg, even.

"Bother me again," I said. "It's good to have someone to talk to."

That's how it all started.

I liked Eliot. It had nothing to do with his looks, although I must admit he was nice to look at.

For one thing, he was a good listener, and you can't say that about many people. But he was also a good talker, and could make me laugh. On my good days, that is. On my bad, he'd sit beside me and we'd talk quietly. Rather, he'd talk and I'd listen, but it took my mind off my poor stomach.

"Look what I brought today," he'd say, hobbling into my room on his crutches. He'd always have something. Maybe it would be a book of crossword puzzles. We liked to do them together. Or he'd read me the entire sports section of the newspaper. I tried to take an intelligent interest in it for his sake. Eliot was very much into sports.

Some days he'd bring a book on tape for us to listen to. His favorite was "Rumpole of the Bailey," and he made me sit through it countless times.

We discovered we both liked Calvin and Hobbes. He had all the cartoon books, and he'd sit in a bedside chair and read them aloud to me. We'd laugh much more than the jokes warranted, I'm sure, but it was nice to be able to laugh again.

I knew Eliot would be going to Hope House when he left the hospital, but I didn't know for how long. When I asked him, he always seemed to change the subject.

I found out why the day he came to say goodbye.

"I'll be waiting for you at Hope House, Beth," he promised.

"Will you be on maintenance or something?" I asked. "I mean, what will be happening to you?"

He didn't say anything for a moment. "I'll be staying there until I find out whether or not I can keep my leg," he replied.

I couldn't believe I'd heard him correctly.

"What . . . what did you say, Eliot?" I asked faintly.

"I said, there's still some doubt whether or not I can keep my leg."

I couldn't speak.

"They caught my cancer pretty early," he explained. "I was one of the lucky ones. The radiation and chemotherapy dealt with the tumor and kept the cancer from spreading—or at least that's what it looks like at this point. Things look pretty good now, but—"

"You mean they might . . . they could . . . ?"

"Yeah. Cheerful thought, isn't it?"

"I don't know what to say, Eliot."

"You don't have to say anything. I can guess what you're thinking. I used to believe that I'd rather be dead than lose a part of myself. Then I got cancer. That's when I realized that if it was a choice between living without a leg or dying with two, I'd choose life."

He picked up his crutches and got to his feet.

"My doctor arranged for me to talk to a couple of his patients who'd undergone amputations. Both of them are sports nuts, just like me. And I'm telling you, Beth, those two guys really taught me something about courage. One of them is still a big skier, although he had to learn new techniques, of course. The other is a cross-country runner."

Eliot leaned toward me, his blue eyes darkening with emotion.

"Ever since I was a little kid I've said I was going to bicycle across the entire United States someday. Well, that's still my goal. And I'm going to do it with two legs or one!"

5

I was glad Eliot would be waiting for me at Hope House when I left the hospital.

It was a lucky thing for me that he'd come into my life right when he did. I'd never needed a close friend as badly as I did at that point.

I did have close girlfriends from school, but it just wasn't the same anymore. We seemed to be living in different worlds. At first I'd gotten a lot of phone calls from them, but after a while the calls began to taper off.

It was partly my fault. I told them the doctor wouldn't allow me to have visitors. That was not exactly true. It's just that I have this thing about people watching me vomit. And then, of course, there was my hair loss. I didn't want them going back to school and telling everyone how terrible poor, pitiful Beth looked.

Pretty soon the calls got fewer and fewer. I

guess they figured that if I couldn't have visitors, phone calls might bother me too.

Finally it was just my best friend, Patti, and a couple of others who were calling regularly. Patti and I had always told each other everything, but now our conversations were awkward and uncomfortable.

"Guess who invited me to the dance next Friday?" Patti said the last time I'd spoken with her.

"Who?"

"George Higgens, that's who!"

I tried to remember George Higgens. Oh yes, the tall, good-looking redhead with the muscles.

"Beth? Are you still there?"

"That's wonderful, Patti. George is really cute."

I tried to sound excited, but my voice dragged. In the past we'd both have shrieked and giggled, but I was tired and dying to take a nap.

I think I hurt Patti's feelings because she said in this wounded tone, "Gee, Beth. This is an incredible break for me, you know. Tara Peters has been chasing him all semester."

"I'm so happy for you, Patti. I'm sorry if I don't sound it. It's just that I'm a little tired right now."

Patti became instantly apologetic. "Oh Beth, of course! I should have known. I mean, I'm so dumb sometimes. So how are you feeling? When you're not tired, that is. How are you *really*?"

Suddenly I felt terribly alone on my end of the

phone. "I'm fine, Patti. It's just that, well, they've given me this stuff to make me sleepy. But I'm fine. Really."

Maybe some people like to talk about how sick they are, but I don't. I knew if I told Patti everything I was going through it would only upset her and make her feel sorry for me, which I didn't want.

There's a terrible gulf between happy people and unhappy ones. You don't realize that until something happens to cast you down into the very depths of depression.

When you're depressed and miserable, you feel as if you're all alone in the world—that you're all by yourself out in the cold, looking through a lighted window where, inside, people are laughing and chatting and going about their cozy, cheery, everyday lives. It's the feeling of being alone that hurts the most—the feeling that no one has any idea what you are going through.

So I was lucky. I wasn't alone. I had Eliot, and he knew what I was going through because he was going through it too.

I especially needed him now. You see, I'd received some bad news about my condition that took my mind, briefly, off losing my hair. It had come as a surprise, too, which made it that much worse.

What had happened was that by the time my

chemo program was completed, I was feeling better and my blood cell count had returned to normal. My family and I thought it would be easy
sailing from here on in.

Dr. Lindberg broke the bad news to us.

"Beth's bone marrow, although improved, remains abnormal," he said.

Mom pressed a hand to her mouth. "What does
that mean, Doctor?" she asked in a strained
voice.

"It means that Beth is in a partial, not a complete remission."

Mom started to interrupt, but Dr. Lindberg
continued on.

"It's hard to evaluate the exact degree of a partial remission of this sort. What it does mean,
though, is that her leukemic cells seem to be
somewhat resistant to the drugs we've used so
far."

"Oh God!" Mom sobbed.

"Is there anything we can do about it?" Dad
asked. I was surprised to hear him speak up. "I
assume there is some further treatment?"

Dr. Lindberg nodded. "Yes, we're going to try
some second-line, experimental drugs on Beth.
We're going to keep trying until we find something that works."

More chemo! I sank back in my bed. How I
dreaded being sick to my stomach again. There's

nothing worse than nausea that never quits. Ask anyone who's ever been seasick.

"When?" I managed to ask. "When do we start?"

"We're going to let your body rest for a few weeks before we begin the next course of chemotherapy," he said. "It's taken quite a beating with this last one. So tomorrow we'll transfer you out to Hope House. I think you're going to like it there."

That's all he told us. More chemotherapy. None of us asked what would happen to me if the new chemotherapy didn't work. Actually, we didn't have to. We all had a pretty good idea. But it was one of those things that neither I nor my family was ready to face. At least, not yet.

Hope House was only about five minutes away from St. Stephen's. It was a large old Victorian mansion that sat back from the road on long, sloping grounds dotted with tall elm trees. It had a pleasant, well-tended look about it that made it seem more like a house than an institution.

It had been six long weeks since I'd last been outdoors. I felt like Rip Van Winkle after his nap.

March had gone out like a lamb that year. The winter snows had long since melted, and tender, pale green shoots had already begun to break through the damp, rich soil of the flower beds that lined the driveway.

It's a good omen, I thought, crossing my fingers. I'd gotten very superstitious lately, and kept looking for good omens in everything. Those eager, sprouting bulbs just *had* to be a good omen. This summer, when the irises are in bloom, I told myself fiercely, I'll be well again.

I looked at Hope House. Once long ago, I guessed, only one family had lived here; one family served and catered to by a small army of servants and gardeners. Now the house had come into its own and was doing public service as a residence and medical facility for seriously ill kids.

According to Dr. Lindberg, about eight kids and four staff members were living in Hope House at the present time. However, a number of kids came to the house for outpatient treatment and counseling, and a large group of staff members—doctors, nurses, counselors, and volunteers—were involved with the house on a daily basis.

Eliot hurried out to greet me and to help me down the steps of the hospital van that had brought me to Hope House. I noticed he was walking much better and only used a cane now.

"Beth? Is that you?" he asked in pretended confusion. "Don't tell me your mother got you into one of those glamorous movie-star wigs she sent for!''

I reached up and patted a cheek curl. "I think it's kind of pretty, actually, but no kid my age wears her hair like this."

What I was thinking, but didn't say aloud, was that no matter what it looked like, it was better than how I appeared without it. The first thing I saw each morning and the last thing I saw at night in the bathroom mirror was my poor, bare-looking head with those awful, tattered wisps of hair—the badge of my disease.

Eliot stepped back and squinted at my head. "You're right. It isn't quite you. But we have a closet full of wigs here. Donated and left-behind ones. You can be a blonde, a brunet, or a redhead. Take your pick. We even have an Al Pacino wig, but that one's for me."

"An *Al Pacino* wig?"

"Well, that's what I call it. It's short with bangs and it looks as if it's been caught in a food processor."

I had to laugh. Eliot looked pleased with himself.

"Come on, Beth. Your room's on the top floor."

Eliot led me into the foyer. At that moment, the door to the right opened and a tall, good-looking man came out. My mother would have called him "distinguished looking." Janna would have said he was the Paul Newman type—Paul Newman being her absolute ideal of a sensational-looking older man.

"Oh-oh, cheez it! The cops!" said Eliot.

"I'm Dr. Graham, the head of Hope House," said the man, extending his hand. "And please don't pay any attention to Eliot. Maybe he'll settle down now that you're here. He's been pacing the floor all morning."

Eliot blushed. I'd never seen him look embarrassed before.

"The reason I've been pacing the floor, in case you want to know," he said, recovering quickly from his blush, "is that I've been trying to walk off Ms. Brady's strawberry pancakes. She forced me to eat too many this morning."

"Ms. Brady is our cook," explained Dr. Graham. "And Eliot is her best customer when it comes to her famous strawberry pancakes. She threatened to chase him off with a stick this morning, as I recall, in spite of what he says."

He gestured toward the door he'd just come through.

"That's the medical wing," he said. "Staff members have their offices and treatment rooms in there. I'm sure that's the last thing you want to see right now, so let me give you a little tour of Hope House and introduce you to some of our staff and residents."

He crossed the broad foyer and opened the door on the opposite side.

"This leads to the communal living area," he said. "We try to keep it separate from the medical wing because it gets pretty noisy in here sometimes."

I found myself in a large, high-ceilinged living room. In spite of the fact that it had been built over a hundred years ago, it was surprisingly cozy and cheerful. Sunlight streamed through the long windows, and potted plants bloomed on side tables. Down-filled sofas with flowered slipcovers and overstuffed chairs had been arranged with the large, marble-manteled fireplace as their focal point. The pleasant smell of a pinewood fire still lingered. I sniffed appreciatively.

"We light a fire in here just about every night," said Dr. Graham. "It's still chilly here in the evenings, and the young people like to pop corn over the fire."

He turned to Eliot. "Alison's coming in tonight. She says she's learned some new songs."

Eliot groaned.

"Alison Kim is our age and is a volunteer here," he explained. "She's a great girl and all that, but I wish she'd never learned to play the guitar. She's always trying to organize a sing-along."

Dr. Graham laughed. It was a pleasant, low laugh.

"Maybe she'll improve if you're patient," he said.

"She's got to get better. She sure can't get any worse," said Eliot.

Dr. Graham's face sobered. "Alison has done volunteer work for us since her little sister Mary was here with Hodgkin's disease," he told me. "Mary died two years ago, but Alison still feels attached to Hope House because Mary was so happy here."

Adjoining the living room was a book-lined library, and beyond that a recreation room with a stereo, comfortable couches, and a large TV.

From there we proceeded into the dining room and kitchen.

Ms. Brady was in the kitchen preparing lunch. From the scent of it, it had to be Italian, and Ms. Brady told us we would be having green pepper steak and mozzarella hoagies. My stomach growled appreciatively. It had been a long time since I'd actually been hungry.

When Ms. Brady saw Eliot, she raised a long wooden spoon in warning.

"Don't you dare touch anything," she snapped.

Eliot assumed a wounded look.

"Why would I?" he asked piteously. "I'm just a

poor, sick kid with the appetite of a bird. I've seen sparrows that eat more than I do."

"Sparrows? Make that vultures," said Ms. Brady, her blue eyes twinkling. "I swear, Eliot, you'd eat road kill if I served it up on a platter!"

Eliot coughed. It was a fake cough, but effective.

"I think my body is trying to make up for all the times I went without meals," he said with a hang-dog look. "When I was on chemotherapy, that is." He coughed again.

Ms. Brady melted.

"I'm having chocolate eclairs for dessert. I'll save you an extra one."

"Shame on you," I whispered as we left the kitchen. "Taking advantage of a nice woman like that!"

"Actually, we have a secret understanding," Eliot said.

"What kind of understanding?"

"That I'm going to marry her as soon as I graduate from high school."

I have a terrible memory for names and faces, and I met a lot of people that morning, but I remembered most of them. That may have been because Eliot told me a little about them later.

First of all, there was Dr. Emily Ambrose. Dr. Ambrose was slim, green-eyed, and romantic looking, with thick chestnut hair. It didn't surprise me when Eliot said he thought she and Dr. Graham were seriously interested in each other.

"Dr. Graham's a widower," he explained later that evening. "His wife died over ten years ago. She was just a young woman, but she had leukemia."

I felt closer to Dr. Graham when I heard that. He'd told me I'd be coming to him for counseling. Now I realized he'd know what I was going through since he'd had firsthand experience of it with a loved one.

Then there was Dr. Lilly Gordon, the oncologist who would be taking over my case while I was at Hope House. Dr. Gordon was around my mother's age, and seemed warmhearted and sensible. She told me she'd be seeing me frequently and monitoring my condition closely.

I also met Ms. McGehan, a nurse with a lovely Irish brogue; and Ben and Andrea Shepherd, a married couple in their early thirties, who did group and family counseling.

"Ms. McGehan and the Shepherds live at Hope House," Dr. Graham explained when he introduced us. "You'll be seeing a lot of them in the future."

There was a crash from the dining room. Someone had just broken some glassware. Lots of it from all the tinkling sounds.

"Rusty!" Ms. McGehan exclaimed.

A tall, lanky redheaded man opened the dining room door and hung his head apologetically.

"Sorry, folks," he said. "I had a little accident, but no one's hurt."

Ms. McGehan put her hands on her hips and shook her head. "It's all those freckles on your face, darlin'. I think they're starting to grow inward and cloud your mind."

Rusty laughed and returned to the dining room, closing the door on his shirttail. He rolled his eyes at us when he opened the door and retrieved it.

"Who was that?" I asked Eliot.

"That's Rusty Feller. He's a part-time nurse here. That klutzy act is mostly genuine, although I suspect he plays it up to make the little kids laugh. He's probably one of the nicest guys I've ever met. Just don't ever go near him if you're carrying a sharp object!"

I was beginning to feel tired by the time we'd toured the ground floor and arrived back at the foyer. The broad, curving stairway leading upward looked endless, and I wondered if I could make it to my floor without someone behind me, pushing all the way. Weeks of lying around in bed had made me lose my land legs, even though the nurses at St. Stephen's had relentlessly driven me to walk up and down the halls every day before my release to Hope House.

Dr. Graham noticed how tired I was.

"I think Beth's had enough for now," he said. "Why don't you show her to her room, Eliot?"

He glanced at his watch.

"I have a staff meeting and I seem to be running late. I'll be up to see you later this afternoon, Beth."

"Come on, Beth," Eliot said, putting his arm around me and letting me lean on him as we went up the stairs. "Don't go getting any funny ideas, though, that I'm going to do this all the time, because I'm not. Ms. Brady would go wacko crazy jealous if she ever saw us like this."

I laughed weakly. "If ego sold for a dollar a pound, Eliot, you'd be an instant multimillionaire."

"What's a muttamiyionaire?" said a little voice from the landing.

There sitting on the floor and watching us from between the balustrades was a little boy in a baseball cap. I fell in love with him on the spot.

He must have been around six years old, because his front teeth were missing. He was thin and as fine-boned as a little bird. His face was all eyes—big, brown eyes. I saw, with a lurch of my heart, that beneath his baseball cap he had no hair.

Another cancer victim. And so young!

"Well, if it isn't Dan the man," Eliot said.

"What are you doing there on the floor? If some-body stepped on you, you'd hardly even leave a grease spot."

The boy giggled and hugged himself delight-edly. "I was spying on you and *her*. She's pretty."

Eliot and I had reached the top of the stairs now and stood on the landing.

"Then let me introduce you," Eliot said with an elegant bow. "Danny, this is Beth. Beth, this is Danny."

In a theatrical aside to me he added, "Danny pretty much rules the roost around here, Beth. You're lucky he likes you. He can be mean and cruel to his enemies."

Danny laughed again. Eliot had an appreciative audience in Danny.

"You're the new one," Danny told me. "They said you were coming."

"News travels fast in the jungle," said Eliot.

"And you're in the girls' wing." Danny pointed down the hall. "I live down there." He pointed in the opposite direction.

"Maybe we'll see each other later at lunch," I said. "And maybe you'll sit next to me since I'm new here and need a friend."

"I will," Danny promised earnestly.

He gave me another heart-stopping look full on from those brown eyes. "I know everybody. I've lived here a lot. Ever since I was this big."

He made a gesture with his hands that indicated something approximately the size of a small rabbit.

He stood watching as Eliot and I walked down the hall to my room.

"What did he mean, he's lived here a lot?" I asked Eliot in a low voice. "Has he been sick long?"

Eliot's usually cheerful face was grim. "He's had leukemia since he was a year old, Beth. Think of it. A year old. It's just not fair!"

"But—but—I don't understand," I said. "Can't they do anything for him?"

Eliot looked at me with a world of sadness in his eyes. "They get him in a state of remission, Beth, and then he has a relapse. Then they get him in remission again and he has another relapse. His remissions have become shorter and shorter."

6

I had a weird dream that night.

I dreamed I was a magician in a circus. There I was in the center ring with the spotlight shining on me. A black-draped table holding a tall silk hat stood next to me.

Suddenly there was a prolonged drumbeat and I reached into the hat. Something warm and furry was wriggling around in there. I took a firm hold on it and pulled it out. It was a white rabbit. No . . . it was someone dressed in a rabbit suit. Danny. I held him straight out before me by his costume ears.

He was just a little rabbit, a miniature one, and he was smiling. Beneath his hood and long white ears he had hair, lots of hair, curly red-gold hair.

Then the spotlight moved and I was left in the dark. There was another drum beat and Eliot appeared. The light followed him as he strode to the center of the ring. He was the ringmaster and wore a fancy red coat and high, polished boots. He seemed pleased about something. Me? No, not me. He wasn't even looking my way. He was gesturing off to the entrance. The spotlight followed his pointing hand and the crowd began to applaud madly. There were whistles and cheers. I wondered who was coming into the ring.

It was Janna. I should have guessed. Janna was wearing a pink ballerina's tutu, spangled tights, and little pink ballet shoes. She was planted firmly and unwaveringly on the back of a prancing white horse. She rode standing up, her hands extended gracefully in acknowledgment of the crowd's cheers. And then she did a typical Janna thing. She waved over in my direction so that I would be included in the crowd's applause.

I woke up, angry and seething, and lay there in the dark grinding my teeth. Even in my dreams, Janna had to come in and steal my spotlight!

It wouldn't require a psychiatrist to interpret this dream, I thought. It was pretty straightforward.

My pique at Janna turned to fear.

What *would* happen when Janna came? Eliot had never been around at St. Stephen's when Janna visited. He had some idea he'd be intruding during visiting hours if he showed up.

But Hope House was different. It was more informal. Eliot was bound to meet Janna. I could see him in my mind's eye—gawking at her and falling madly under her spell.

True, Janna was older than Eliot, but that wouldn't make any difference to him. Besides, it was the principle of the thing that mattered to me. Eliot was my friend. And I didn't want Janna to mess up a very precious friendship.

If I knew Janna, she'd probably be happy that I had a good friend like Eliot. That was what was so aggravating about her. You couldn't even hate her without feeling like a rat.

I flopped over in bed and gave the pillow a hard thump.

Then it dawned on me that I was behaving like a fool. Here I was, getting all worked up in the middle of the night because I'd dreamed that Eliot was a ringmaster in a circus and that he'd clapped for Janna in her pink tutu.

I almost laughed aloud, and then thought, yeah, Beth, keep laughing. And just you wait until Eliot meets Janna. There you'll be again, on the outside looking in.

In the next bed, my roommate stirred.

I'd met her at lunch yesterday. Was it yesterday still? I peered at the luminous hands of my bedside clock. It was three o'clock in the morning.

I remembered a quote I'd read once. It was something the writer F. Scott Fitzgerald once said. He suffered from insomnia and would wake up in the middle of the night all the time and worry about things—things like his writer's block and his poor wife, Zelda, who was in a mental institution. Anyway, he said, "In the dark night of the soul it's always 3:00 A.M." I knew just what he meant.

My roommate mumbled something unintelligible and flopped around again.

Her name was Rachel. Rachel Harris. She had anorexia nervosa. Her hair was long and black and her skin was pale. She was skeleton thin with knobbly little collarbones and tiny wrists. She told me she was recovering from her eating disorder, though, and was actually starting to put on a little weight.

"I have to fight the thought that I look like a fat pig, though. That's part of my problem, you know."

I liked Rachel, once I got past all her fussy, prissy little mannerisms. I mean, when your roommate has taken a piece of chalk and drawn a line down the middle of the room and told you to keep your things on your side because she had hers arranged just so on her side . . . well, that sort of thing makes it hard to love someone right off the bat. But we'd had to read about eating disorders in health and hygiene class, and I remembered learning that anorexics tend to be perfectionists, so I figured I could get along with Rachel just fine as long as she stayed on her side of the room with her dumb piece of chalk.

I turned over as quietly as possible and tried to go back to sleep. Heaven forbid I rouse Rachel. She might want to leap out of bed and tidy up.

Then I guess I must have fallen asleep because suddenly it was morning.

As it turned out, I didn't have to worry long about what would happen when Eliot met Janna. It happened that very afternoon.

When Mom phoned to say she and Janna would be by right after Janna's last class, I invited Eliot to wait for them with me in the living room of Hope House. I figured I might as well get the fateful meeting over with as quickly as possible. No sense sitting around stewing.

All morning I'd been feeling hateful toward Eliot in advance. I was sure he was going to act like a total fool over Janna. Silly as it sounds, I still couldn't forgive him for what he did as the ringmaster of my dream circus—taking the spotlight away from me and my magician's act and giving it to Janna on her white horse.

Janna came in, looking like Miss Teenage America.

I glanced quickly, defensively, over at Eliot to see his reaction. He looked pleasant but not goopy. Friendly but not star struck. My heart soared in my body. I should have guessed Eliot would pass the Janna test. Well, it wasn't my fault. It was the fault of that crazy dream.

How untrusting of me, I thought. Where was my faith and confidence? Naturally he was much too sensible to fall madly in love with an older woman, no matter how irresistible she was. Why didn't I think of that at three o'clock this morning?

When I introduced Eliot to Mom and Janna, he behaved like a real charmer. I was proud of him. He told me later his older brother used to tell him how to act around a girl's parents. He had it down pretty pat.

"I can see why Beth is so good looking," he told Mom. "It sure does run in the family. You must have married young, Mrs. Manning. You don't look old enough to have daughters this age."

Now that is probably the oldest bamboozle in the world. Adam must have said it to Eve. But Eliot sounded sincere.

"Why, thank you, Eliot." Mom blushed and, fortunately, managed not to simper. Just yesterday she'd been moaning about crow's-feet and cellulite.

"Beth is lucky to have a friend like you, Eliot," Janna said. "She told us how good you were to her, and how much you helped her when she was at St. Stephen's."

And that was all Janna said about *me*. The rest of her conversation was about all the extracurricular activities she'd just rushed out and signed up for.

It was weird. She didn't talk about her classes the way she usually does, and Janna is a serious student. No, just about these activities she'd never been particularly interested in before, like the Prom Hostess Club and the Social Committee and the Up-With-Somerset-High Society.

"But Janna," I said, "you've always said you weren't interested in being a busy bee, pom-pom-girl type. You said the poetry club and the chess club were more your speed."

"Well, I've changed my mind, Bethie."

Janna's eyes had sort of a flat, evasive look when they met mine—you know, that wide open blank look we all use when we're fibbing.

She and Mom didn't stay long.

Janna glanced at her watch and jumped to her feet.

"Look at the time! I've got a Social Committee meeting. We're planning the spring formal. I'll just make it if we leave now."

Even though I'd dreaded her coming and her meeting Eliot, now that she was standing there shuffling her feet impatiently, I felt miffed and cheated. What was her hurry? Why didn't she want to stay and tenderly minister to me, her poor, sick little sister? And what on earth was all this new after-school activity stuff?

Mom, though, kept up her bubbling optimistic chatter until the door closed on her.

"You look wonderful, Bethie! Much better than last week. Rest up, now, because these new chemo treatments are going to do the trick. As a matter of fact, I'd better get busy finding a tutor for you this summer so you'll be ready to rejoin your old class next September. Aren't you looking forward to going back to school again?"

Sometimes I wished she'd just give it a rest. There was so much ahead of me before I could think of living a normal life again. School seemed like a million years away. I wanted so badly to be able to talk to Mom about how I felt and what my fears were, but whenever I tried she'd cut me off with some trite quote about thinking positively. There must be at least five hundred positive-thinking quotes and Mom seemed to know every one of them.

After they left, I walked over to the fireplace and inspected myself in the mirror that hung above it. I couldn't help but grimace at my reflection.

I'd rummaged around in the wigs closet that morning and come up with a sixties-era flower-child hairdo. It was long, straight, and blond with Prince Valiant bangs. I wore it with a pink headband. I'd figured that if I had to compete with Janna, I ought to strive for a poignant, waiflike effect. A mistake. I don't have the coloring or features for a blond, waiflike flower child.

Eliot watched me making faces at myself in the mirror.

"You know, Beth," he finally said, "I hate to tell you this, but, pretty as you are, you look a lot like a witch in that wig."

"Really, Eliot! Thanks a lot!"

"Why don't you just go wigless?"

"For the simple fact that I'd be bald without one. Well, nearly bald."

"So what? Isn't there some gorgeous model who shaves her head?"

"Yeah, but on her it looks terrific."

"So why not on you too, Beth? Or do you have a pointy green Martian head that you're hiding?"

"My head is not green and pointy. Nevertheless, I would prefer not to reveal it," I replied with great dignity.

Eliot mulled that over for a long moment. Then suddenly he said, "Let's have a party!"

"What?"

"Haven't you ever seen any of those old Judy Garland and Mickey Rooney movies on TV?" he asked.

"Of course. They show them all the time on the late, late show. But what's that got to do with my wearing a wig?"

"Well, whenever things go wrong in those movies, Mickey always saves the day by saying, 'Let's have a show!' "

I shook my head in bewilderment. "First you said a party, Eliot. Now you're talking about a show. I wish you'd make up your mind." I grinned. "What there is of it, that is."

"But we don't have enough talent at Hope House for a show. It will have to be a party."

"Have I missed something important in this conversation?" I said. "What are we talking about? What does Mickey Rooney have to do with us?"

Eliot waved me to the sofa and sat down beside me. He leaned forward eagerly, his blue eyes sparkling.

"When I saw you making faces at yourself just now," he said, "I realized what was wrong with all of us here at Hope House."

"You're telling me that you just now noticed the fact that we're all *sick*?" I asked in disbelief.

"No, dummy. What I mean is that all of us here have problems that make us look, well, different from healthy kids."

"That's for sure," I agreed.

"And the strange way we look makes us as miserable as our diseases do."

I thought about that for a while. Eliot was right. Looking peculiar to a kid was every bit as terrible as feeling awful.

Then I thought about all the kids living at Hope House that I'd met yesterday:

Anorexic Rachel, pale and bone-thin, looking like a bean pole but feeling, she said, like the fat lady in a circus. Now there was real double trouble.

Pretty Lydia, with curvature of the spine. She'd had surgery and was now in a back brace. Lydia was afraid her old friends would dump her for looking like "a geek." Those were her words, not mine. Personally, I didn't think much of her old "friends."

Steve, who had muscular dystrophy and was a prisoner to his wheelchair. He told me how tired he was of people staring at him in restaurants and stores.

And then there was Carrie with the gorgeous blond hair. She'd lost a leg to bone cancer and was waiting for an artificial limb. Carrie told me wistfully that she'd never look good in a bikini again. I told her she'd look good in anything, but I don't think I convinced her.

Then Eliot, of course, and me and Danny—my Danny—with his old man's head and baseball cap. No one was going to make him feel ashamed of his appearance. Not while I was around!

"Yes," I said slowly. "I guess you can say that we all have a few self-image problems, Eliot."

"Exactly!" he said. "That's why I think it's a great idea to have a party."

"Why?" I asked. "What's so magical about having a party?"

"Because," he said, enunciating every word, "this is going to be a costume party. We're going to come as ourselves. We're going to let it all hang out, Beth, and to heck with looking different. And we're going to have fun doing it too—probably the only fun a lot of us have had in a long time. And maybe we'll all feel better about ourselves afterward too."

"A costume party? I can't even think how I'd come, Eliot."

I got up and drifted over to the mirror.

"If we're supposed to let it all hang out, I guess that means I will have to go without my wig. Well, at least I'll be comfortable. This stupid thing is hot and itchy."

I turned my head from side to side and squinted at myself slantwise.

"I could always come as Humpty Dumpty, I guess."

"Aren't you a little skinny for Humpty?"

"Yeah, besides it's not a glamorous look. I want to look . . . exotic! Yes, that's it. Exotic."

I peered at my image more intently. With lots of makeup, especially eye makeup and a few safety pins glued to my ear lobes, I could pass for a punk rocker.

"How about me coming as a punk rocker?" I asked. "You can too. We'll be a matched pair. And I'll have to find something cute for Danny to wear. Maybe he could come as a Munchkin. And . . ."

I turned my back on my reflection and faced Eliot.

"So what does Judy always say?"

"What?"

"When Mickey Rooney says, 'Let's have a show,' " I explained patiently, "what does Judy Garland say?"

Eliot wrinkled his forehead. "I think she says, 'Oh jeepers, what a swell idea,' or words to that effect. And then she rounds up the gang."

I pasted a bright, expectant smile on my face. "Oh jeepers, Mickey! What a swell idea or words to that effect! Yes, let's have that party!"

Then, arm in arm, Eliot and I left the living room to round up the gang.

7

The party was a smash success.

Getting permission to hold it was no problem. The staff was wildly supportive. Almost too supportive. Something like this had never been done before at Hope House, so all the staff members rushed up eagerly and volunteered to help in every way possible.

Eliot and I had to explain tactfully that it was important to us kids that we did everything for the party ourselves. This was supposed to be strictly a kid thing, we told them. Adults would be included by invitation only.

We did, though, take Ms. Brady up on her offer to do the catering for the party. In the first place, she forbade anyone to set foot in her sacred kitchen on pain of death. In the second, she swore she'd feed us her dreaded and awful mystery meat loaf (Ms. Brady's one and only cooking

shortcoming) every night forever if we didn't let
her try out her party recipes on us.

And Ben and Andrea Shepherd, the social
workers who lived at Hope House, said they
would help us with the special lighting and the
sound system. They were a nice couple, fun and
helpful, and were always ready to lend a hand.

Once those details were settled, we started
thinking about decorations and costumes. I didn't
mean to tell people how I planned to come, but it
slipped out, and everyone thought my coming as
a punk rocker was a great idea. So great, in fact,
that they all decided to make this not just an ordinary costume party, but a celebrity costume
party, with everyone coming as his or her favorite
celebrity. It didn't have to be a real celebrity. It
could be a fictional one, or even a made-up one.

Since we were all short on cash, decorations
would have to be kept simple and inexpensive. We
figured balloons would be okay, but most of us
drew the line at crepe paper streamers.

"Too grade schoolish," Rachel said firmly. "We
need something more sophisticated."

Steve came up with the perfect idea. He leaned
back in his wheelchair and folded his hands on
his stomach.

"Posters," he said. "Let's put posters of celebri-
ties on the walls."

That worked out well. A lot of us had posters on

our bedroom walls at home that we could have our folks bring in, and we took up a quick collection for a few new ones. There was a poster store in Somerset, only a couple of blocks from Hope House.

Then we opened up the floor for discussion on what the poster committee would buy.

"I like Bart Simpson," Steve said. "How about one of him?"

"Really, Steve," Lydia said. "A cartoon character?"

Lydia was the girl in the back brace. She'd told us earlier that she planned to major in art in college. "I've seen a great one of van Gogh after he cut off his ear. Now there's a real celeb. He looks nice and melancholy in it too. Nobody ever bought any of his pictures while he was alive, you know."

"How disgusting," Rachel said. "Does it show the bloody stump?"

"No, of course not," said Lydia. "It shows him from the other side. But he looks real sad. Kind of like the solitary genius he was."

"That ought to put us in a swinging party mood," Steve said. "Way to go, van Gogh!"

"Okay then, you suggest someone," snapped Lydia.

Eliot hastily intervened. "I make a motion that

we leave the selection of the new posters to the poster committee. All in favor . . ."

The poster committee was made up of Steve, Rachel, and Alan Schmidt. Alan came in for physical therapy a couple of times a week. He'd been in a terrible car accident and had undergone surgery and then had been in a cast for a long time. He still had a bad limp.

We'd opened up the party to outpatients like Alan because, although they didn't live at Hope House, they were still a part of it and had the same worries about body image and the future as we did. We'd also invited Alison Kim, the teen-aged volunteer, because she'd become a real part of the gang. There would be about twenty of us, total, at the party.

Ms. McGehan, the nurse with the Irish brogue, drove the poster committee to the shop in her van. Rusty Feller went with them, to help get Steve in and out of his wheelchair. Rusty volunteered to drive but was shouted down.

"There seems to be a slight lack of confidence around here concerning my driving ability," he said. "I'll have you know that behind the wheel I drive as skillfully as James Bond himself."

The recreation room looked absolutely super the night of the party. We'd done an outstanding job of decorating. The posters looked great on the pine-paneled walls and set the mood for the party.

Fresh flowers were everywhere, courtesy of Rachel's father who's a florist. Music played softly on the stereo, and fat colorful candles in hurricane shades burned brightly on every flat surface.

The Ping-Pong table was covered with an embroidered cloth and upon it Ms. Brady, in a high state of nerves, laid out the finest products of her labors.

We all knew she'd been locked in her kitchen cooking away madly the last couple of days, but we weren't prepared for the huge selection of party foods she'd done up for us. There were yummy fillings baked in delicate golden phyllo pastry, meatballs in sweet-and-sour sauce, egg rolls with hot mustard, sliced ham, roast beef, chicken, and much, much more. She'd cooked up enough food to feed a small army and somehow, surprisingly, most of it disappeared before the party ended.

We'd fixed up one end of the room as a small stage for the entertainment portion of the party. This came toward the end of the evening, and we'd invited the adult staff members to join us for this part.

The rules were that anyone who wanted to sing, recite, or do a lip-sync number was welcome to do so. We had a surprising number of takers.

Rachel and Alison Kim came as twin versions of Cher. Alison had found a long, black wig that matched Rachel's hair, and they wore black tights and tunics and lots of eye makeup. Although Rachel was tall and thin and Alison was short and square, they called themselves "Cher and Cher Alike" and sang that old Sonny and Cher number, "I've Got You, Babe"; only they changed it to, "We've got you guys," meaning all of us at Hope House. It was very touching, actually, that they felt that way.

I was pleased with the costumes I'd put together for Danny and his roommate, Alex. Alex was seven and awaiting a kidney transplant. He had to go on dialysis three times a week, but was up and about for the party.

I'd dressed them as Munchkins from the *Wizard of Oz* movie, in little caps and striped knee socks and oversized green T-shirts. Then I taught them that song the three members of the Munchkin Lollipop Guild sing to Dorothy: "We welcome you to Munchkin Land." It was short and easy for them to remember, and I also taught them a couple of shuffle-tap dance steps. They brought down the house.

When everyone clapped and stamped, Danny put his little hands in front of his face and peeped out through his fingers. That made everyone clap even harder.

Steve did a one-man comedy routine. He came dressed in tennis clothes with a big "Play Wheelchair Tennis" sign across the back of his chair. He pretended he was Andre Agasi grown middle-aged and arthritic, and that he was due at the courts for mixed wheelchair doubles with Ivan Lendl, Steffi Graf, and Martina Navratilova.

"He could go on the stage as a comedian," Alan said. "He's really good."

We repeated the compliment to Steve when he joined us later at the refreshment table. It seemed to be a new idea to him, one that gave him something to think about.

"Well, why not?" Steve asked, half to himself. "There's a blind, stand-up comic. Why not a sighted, sit-down comic?"

I made my first totally hairless appearance that evening. I took the fateful plunge and cut off the remaining bits of fuzz. It was a traumatic experience, but when I was finished I looked a lot better than I had with all the trailing wisps. Then I laid on makeup with a heavy hand and dressed in the weirdest, tackiest assortment of clothes I could find. I finished by gluing a big safety pin to my right ear.

I called myself Delilah. Eliot was Samson, and dressed to match me. We were a pair of fabulous pop singers, we said. A hairless Samson and a bald Delilah.

We did a rap lip-sync thing to a record. Well, Eliot did the rap thing, while I danced around behind him as his backup performer.

While I was dancing, a funny thing happened. I realized that for the first time since my chemotherapy, I felt comfortable about my appearance. Maybe it was because everyone else at the party had similar problems, and no one stared at me and wondered what was wrong with me.

I could tell I wasn't the only one who felt this way. The others were also, as Eliot had said, being themselves only more so.

Even Lydia, who was usually vain about her appearance, didn't try to disguise her back brace. Normally she wore baggy tops with high collars and floppy jackets to hide the fact that she was braced erect from hips to neck.

She'd come to the party as Madonna, and wore shorts, black fishnet stockings, and one of those corsetty-looking tops that Madonna is famous for, only Lydia openly wore her back brace over it, as if she didn't care what anyone thought of it—or her.

She looked every bit as pretty—more so, actually—as a pop star. Maybe because it was the first time I'd ever seen her laughing and looking completely happy. She had a sort of glow about her that completely altered her appearance.

The high point of the entertainment came at the end, when Carrie sang.

Carrie had lost a leg to bone cancer. She came as Peter Pan—the boy who lived in Never-Never Land and refused to grow up.

She sang "I'm Flying," from Disney's *Peter Pan*. In the film, Peter is teaching Wendy and her brothers how to fly. Flying, he says, is merely a case of mind over matter. Think of a beautiful thought, any lovely thought, he tells them in song, and you can fly!

It was just a simple little song. For children, really. So why did I stand there with a lump in my throat as Carrie's pure, clear soprano soared high and true around me?

She stood there in the spotlight, leaning on her crutches. The empty leg of her green tights was rolled up and pinned to the bottom of her fringed tunic. Her remaining leg was slim and pretty.

Carrie looked out over the audience with fear- less eyes that looked squarely into the future and accepted what they saw there.

What she was trying to tell us was that none of us were chained to the ground. That we could— all of us—fly and soar if we set our minds to it. It was up to us, she was saying, and the beauty of her message and voice nearly knocked the socks off everyone present.

When she'd finished, the applause was subdued, but several of us were knuckling our eyes. Over in a corner, Dr. Graham was blowing his nose, and Ben and Andrea Shepherd had their arms around each other. Ms. McGehan, who was hardly the discreet type, ran over and hugged Carrie.

Later, after everyone had gone to bed, Eliot and I sat in the rubble of the rec room and talked.

"Did you notice, Eliot, that all the kids seem a lot closer to each other now than they did before we started to plan our party?"

Eliot laughed. "Yeah. I heard Rachel and Steve having a real argument over something. Before, they'd been only polite acquaintances. Now they're family, and can argue like family."

"So it was the party?" I asked. "Can planning a party bring people together like that? I mean, make them feel like family?"

Eliot thought for a while. "Not normally, I guess. But let's face it, Beth. None of us here at Hope House is exactly normal. We've all got special problems, and we're just about the only people who understand what we're going through."

"You're right," I admitted, thinking of how hard a time I'd been having lately when I tried to talk normally to my family.

There was another silence. Then Eliot said, "Lifeboat comradery, that's what it's called."

"What? What did you say, Eliot?"

"Lifeboat comradery. It's the term for a special type of closeness people share when they've been through a dangerous experience, like being cast adrift in a lifeboat, and they have to depend on each other. Or like men who have been in combat together. They share something unique."

"I see," I said thoughtfully. "And you're saying that's what's happening here at Hope House?"

"Yes." Eliot nodded. "It's as if we're all in a lifeboat and we're pulling together because we need each other and we're all determined to be survivors."

"Survivors," I said. "I hope that's what we'll be, every one of us. Survivors."

8

Later, looking back on it, the party reminded me of an old-fashioned Mardi Gras, where everyone dresses up and has a good time because the mournful season of Lent is about to begin.

A sort of Lenten season began for me soon after the party.

During one of my checkups, Dr. Gordon, the Hope House oncologist, told me I'd be going to St. Stephen's Hospital to begin my new chemotherapy treatments in a couple of weeks.

And how I dreaded it! One reason was, of course, because of the awful nausea and fatigue that went with the treatments. But what had really begun to scare me—scare me blue—was the knowledge that this next course of treatments was *IT*! If they couldn't get me in a state of complete remission this time, I'd have to face the fact that I just might not live to that ripe old age everybody talks about.

I'd never really thought about dying before. I'd seen it in the movies and on television, but I'd never connected it to me. I figured it happens to everyone someday, but I didn't have to worry about that for a long, long time. Or so I'd thought.

And now here I was, fourteen years old, facing the possibility that the person who was me, Beth Manning, might soon disappear from the world, like a burning candle when it's snuffed out, leaving a swift and sudden darkness.

It helped that I'd begun going to Dr. Graham for psychotherapy. At first I fought the idea. I thought only psychos needed that sort of thing.

It turned out to be nothing at all like I'd imagined, though, and I began to look forward to my sessions with him.

He didn't make me lie on a couch and rehash my earliest childhood memories. Mainly we'd just sit and talk about me and how I felt about things —all sorts of things, not just my leukemia, although, of course, that was discussed a great deal.

What I liked most about Dr. Graham was that he didn't tell me what I should or shouldn't think, or where I was making a mistake, the way most adults do when they talk to you. No, he just let me talk, asking a question every now and then that made me stop and analyze my feelings about something.

I felt sometimes as if I were bouncing my thoughts against him, the way a beginning tennis player hits practice shots to an instructor. And my thoughts always seemed to come back to me straight and true, the way a practice ball hit by a pro comes back to an amateur.

Naturally with all this talking, the problem of my jealousy of Janna came spilling out. When I told him about it, I peeped up at him from under my eyelashes, fearing his disapproval. He'd met Janna, and anyone who meets her, even for the first time, sees what a good, loving person she is. So how would he feel about me, rat fink that I was?

Dr. Graham wasn't shocked or disapproving. "Sibling rivalry," he told me, "has been around for as long as there have been siblings."

"Yeah. Look at Cain and Abel," I said.

"You've picked an extreme case," he said, laughing. "I hardly think, Beth, that you are in the same league as Cain."

Then we talked about jealousy and what a destructive emotion it is, and how it hurts the jealous party. We ended our session with him giving me a book of old Russian short stories. There was one story in the collection, he said, that he wanted me to read so we could discuss it the next time we met.

The story was about a group of bedridden men in a hospital ward. One man's bed was by a window. It was the only window in the ward, and all the others resented the fact that *he* got the window.

But the man by the window was kind and good. All day long he'd entertain the others by telling them all the beautiful things he was seeing from that window. He'd describe children at play and the trees and flowers and changing seasons.

This made the others even more jealous. They contrived that he wouldn't receive medical help when he most needed it, and so the man by the window died and another took his place.

The new man could hardly wait to see all the wonderful things from that window. And so, the next morning, the sun came up and he looked eagerly from the window and saw . . . an ugly blank wall.

Those old nineteenth-century Russians could really tell a story. I put the book down, struck to the heart, and cried.

There was so much of me in those awful, jealous old men, and something of Janna in the man who'd tried to make life more beautiful for the others.

And that's exactly what jealousy gets you, I

thought, a miserable, depressing look at an ugly blank wall. Deep down maybe I'd always known this, but I'd never expressed the thought clearly to myself before.

I remembered something an English teacher once said: "A good writer takes a powerful emotion and crystallizes it into words."

That's what that Russian writer had done. Dr. Graham and I discussed the story and my reaction to it at my next therapy session.

"And so, Doctor," I concluded happily, "I'm never going to be jealous of Janna again."

Dr. Graham smiled. "I'm afraid it's not quite that simple, Beth. You can't turn off a strong emotion like jealousy that easily."

"No? Then what am I supposed to do?"

"Continue in the direction you're headed now. You've taken the first step. You've faced your problem squarely and honestly. You've seen how destructive your jealousy is to you and how unfair to your sister. Your mind has accepted all this. And now, little by little, your emotions will too. But jealousy is a habit, and you can't break a habit in one afternoon."

Dr. Graham was right. My mind knew I was dead wrong to think, "Why not *her*?" the next few times I saw Janna's thick black hair shining in the lamplight, and I was sure my next course of chemo would destroy the bits of fuzz that were starting to appear on my head.

My mind knew I was wrong, that is, but my stomach would get that familiar chewing sensation that told me my inner devil was still alive and doing his old jealousy thing.

So I learned to stop and deliberately make myself remember that Russian story and visualize the ugly wall which is the only reward of a jealous heart. And soon, sooner than I'd expected, in just a matter of days actually, I found myself feeling better. Happier, cleaner, kind of scoured out inside or something. It's hard to describe the feeling, but everyone has had it at one time or another. It's like when you do the right thing, or give someone a wonderful present, or say something to lift someone out of a fit of the blues. That sort of feeling.

I knew I was on the right track at last!

The ironic part was that now that I was beginning to behave like a normal person again, it was Janna—beautiful, wonderful Janna—who was starting to act weird.

9

We were seeing Dr. Graham as a family now too.

There's a play the local high school did last year called *You Can't Take It With You*. It was about this wild, flaky family. If any group of people needed psychological counseling, that bunch did. Compared to them, my family was normal as blueberry pie. Or at least that's what Mom said.

So again . . . *again*, Dr. Graham patiently explained the "why" of our regular family sessions, that family therapy did *not* mean anyone was behaving bizarrely.

"An experience as traumatic as cancer can affect the entire family," he told us. "No family member is going to go through this unchanged. My goal is to see that the change is for the better."

He went on to tell us that the family needed to be a healing unit for the cancer patient—that all its members had to pull together. And that, he said, required open communication.

Oboy, I thought. He's just put his finger on the broken button. If I need open communication in my family to get better, I might as well throw in the sponge right now.

It was almost impossible to talk to Mom these days. As I've said before, her way of dealing with my leukemia was to keep telling me everything was coming up roses, and to refuse to discuss what would happen if this next series of chemotherapy treatments didn't get me into a complete remission.

Yes, talking to her was frustrating, but at least she *talked*. Dad was like The Great Stone Face. All that stiff-upper-lip stuff sounds noble and inspiring in books, but it's hard to take in real life.

Then, of course, there was Janna. Or rather, there *wasn't* Janna.

My sister was missing most of our family therapy sessions. She was involved at school with more and more extracurricular activities to the point that I hardly saw her anymore. When she did come, she'd fidget and look edgy and strained and talk only about "safe" subjects like boys and school.

Janna came over, alone, to see me one afternoon when we weren't scheduled for family therapy. I think she planned it that way so she could playact without getting caught.

I took her into the living room. It was empty and quiet. The smell of last night's pine fire still lingered, and the afternoon sun, slanting in through the oriel window, lent a golden cast to the room.

After we'd talked a long time about absolutely nothing, I made a stab at a little open communication.

"You don't come here very often, Janna," I said.

Janna rose, avoiding my eyes, and moved restlessly to the window where she stood, back to me, fiddling with the drapery pull. She didn't answer.

How do you communicate with someone's back, I wondered angrily. How do you make someone answer who doesn't want to?

"I wish you'd talk to me, Janna."

A little while ago I'd have been glad not to have to see and talk to my sister, glad to escape that *why me, why not her*? feeling. But now I was trying to do the right thing. I didn't know what was going to happen to me in the coming days and I wanted us, Janna and me, to have again what we once had together.

I wish I could have said it like that, straight out, but the words were all jumbled in my mind and I couldn't jar them loose.

Instead I said, "Janna? Did you hear what I said?"

She turned from the window reluctantly and with a sigh.

"Yes, Beth, I heard you."

She drifted back to the armchair she'd been sitting in and made a big ceremony out of plumping up its cushion before answering my question.

"The reason I don't come as often as I'd like is because there's so much going on at school," she said finally. "You'll see what I mean when you're a senior and are rushing around in all directions too."

"But you never come to family therapy," I said.

She sat down. "I just don't think it's necessary, that's all. We're a normal, well-adjusted family, so who needs therapy?"

"We do, Janna," I insisted stubbornly. "All of us."

Janna tossed her head. Her black hair went flying. "Well, I don't. Besides, you'll be starting chemo again soon and after that you'll come home and everything will be fine again."

After she left, I lay there thinking: She's wrong. She must realize that nothing in our family will ever be the same again after this. Not ever.

* * *

Dr. Graham tried to explain Janna's behavior to Mom, Dad, and me when we next met for therapy.

"It isn't that Janna doesn't love you anymore, Beth. On the contrary. The way she's acting shows she cares very much."

"How do you figure that, Doctor?" I asked.

"Her behavior is a classic example of denial," he replied. "And denial is a form of grief. Janna is so terrified of losing you that she's backing away and trying to pretend a problem doesn't exist. . . ."

I didn't understand that. I didn't understand it at all.

"Can't Janna see I need her now?" I argued.

"Aren't you being unreasonable?" asked Mom. "Janna has always mothered and spoiled you. And now, when she's hurting, aren't you expecting too much of her?"

She was careful to make it a question, not a statement, in keeping with one of the ground rules Dr. Graham had laid down in the beginning.

"No," I said flatly. "I only expect her to come and see me every once in a while."

Dr. Graham intervened. "I'd like us to continue this discussion another time," he said, "when Beth has had a chance to think over what I mentioned about Janna's behavior being a form of grief. Perhaps when she looks at it from a different perspective . . ."

That's how our therapy went. It helped to clear the air a lot, although, even after thinking over what Dr. Graham said about Janna, I still couldn't understand why she was acting so peculiar.

Mom was surprised when I told her how I felt about her cheerleader attitude.

"It's scaring me," I said. "Whenever you act like that, there's always something terrible you're hiding. I mean, like when you dented the car fender that time, and you came home acting like Beaver Cleaver's mother doing one of her perfect wifey routines."

Mom frowned. "Really, Beth! How can you—"

Then she caught herself and thought quietly for a moment. We weren't supposed to snap back at each other. We were supposed to carefully think over what the other family member had said.

"Me? A cheerleader?" she said slowly. "Maybe that's what I've been, but isn't that what I've always been, what a mother does to keep everyone moving forward?"

"Well yes, Mom, but you've been so . . . so whacked out about it."

I don't know if Mom heard me. Almost to herself she said, "When you were little and came to me with a bump, I'd kiss it to make it well and then play a game with you to make you forget the hurt. 'Momma, fix it!' you used to say."

She put her fingers to her eyes.

"So I guess that's what I've been trying to do now. The kissing didn't make it well. Now I'm playing a game to make the hurt go away."

From behind the fingers, crooked paths of tears, like rain on a windowpane, ran down her cheeks.

"Oh, how I wish I could fix it this time, Bethie."

We all cried then. Even Dad.

People talk about "good" cries. "I had a good cry," they'll say. I never knew a cry could be good before. A cry is a sad thing, I always thought, not good.

This was a good cry.

The next time we met, we talked about how we felt about Dad's silence, his stiff-upper-lip thing.

It was Mom who led into it, not me.

"It makes me feel so alone, George," she said. "If only you would *talk* to me. Say something. Let me know how you feel."

It took a long time to squeeze it out of him, with both Mom and me begging him to tell us what was going on in his head.

And something definitely was going on inside Dad's head. Something big enough to make that vein in his forehead a permanent fixture. Mom said his stomach ulcer was acting up too. She said he was going through Maalox like it was soda pop.

Finally Dad opened up. It was hard for him, he said, to express his feelings.

Mom rolled her eyes dramatically at that, but a glance from Dr. Graham settled her down pretty fast.

"I guess I've felt I had to be the strong one for everyone's sake," he said.

"But you can be strong and talk too," I said. "You're my father. I need to know how you feel about things."

Well, it went on like that for a long time, with Dad hanging on like a bulldog to the belief that real men don't cry, complain, moan, bare their feelings, or express fear.

As Dr. Graham told me before, no one can change overnight. Dad will never be a model for the New Age sharing, communicative male, but at least he was opening up a little—not much, but a little—now that he'd come to realize how important it was to Mom and me. He told me now what I'd always known, but what I needed to hear from him: that he loved me and would give everything he had in the world, including his own good health, to make me well again.

Mom and Dad had their arms around each other when they left the office that day.

Dr. Graham told us something that seemed almost unbelievable, particularly because of the way my folks were drawing closer and closer together now. He said that in some cases, childhood cancer actually causes the parents to separate, that it can split a marriage right down the middle the way a bolt of lightning splits a living tree.

Well, it wasn't going to happen to *my* family! We had a lot of love going for us, and now we were beginning to understand each other better than we ever had before.

It was like what Eliot had said about *lifeboat comradery*. My parents and I were sharing a terrible experience, but we were sharing it openly and honestly now, and we would be survivors, one way or the other.

And Janna? What about Janna? Had she changed?

No, she was still acting weird and doing her denial bit. I was the one who had to change. As Dr. Graham said, "You can't change other people. You can only change your way of reacting to them."

I came to understand how Janna felt and loved her in spite of—no, make that *because of*—her denial. It showed she loved me enough that she couldn't bear the thought of my dying, didn't it? And hadn't she been willing to put up with my crazy behavior the past year and a half? The least I could do in return was put up with hers.

I wish I could say I felt this way because I'd thought things through sensibly and maturely, and began to understand and accept what Janna was doing.

It didn't happen that way. I'm not that wise or mature. I had to stand in her shoes before I saw where she was coming from.

And that was because of Danny. Little Danny. My Danny.

What happened was that Danny started to go downhill. Eliot had once tried to tell me Danny wasn't going to be one of the lucky ones, but I wouldn't listen. I acted just like Janna. I kept denying the fact that Danny was going to die.

10

I don't know why I felt the way I did about Danny or why he was so special to me.

Maybe I thought of him as my dream child, the little boy I might never live long enough to have. Or maybe it was because he seemed so fragile and breakable and I couldn't help feeling protective of him. Or maybe it was the way he looked at me with those big, trusting eyes.

Whatever it was, it was mutual.

After that first day, Danny followed me around like a little shadow. When we walked in the garden, he'd put his little hand in mine just as though we'd always walked that way together. His hand was so tiny and thin. I could feel every bird-frail bone, and I was always careful not to squeeze it too hard for fear of breaking it.

He seemed to sense my fear.

"You can hold my hand hard, Beth," he'd say. "You can't hurt it."

"But I'm holding it hard, Danny," I'd fib. "I guess I just don't have a very strong grip."

"That's 'cause you're a girl," he'd say happily. "I'm a boy. When I'm a big boy, I'm going to have neato muscles like Eliot's."

Eliot was his number two favorite. I, of course, was number one.

Whenever you asked Danny how he was, instead of saying "fine" like everyone else, he'd always say, "Oh, better." Only he pronounced it *beddo*.

"Hi, Danny. How are you?"

"Oh, beddo."

It nearly broke my heart to think that here was a little kid who'd been so sick all his life that just feeling better was good news.

After the celebrity party, he seemed to admire me even more. He thought I was awfully smart the way I fixed him and Alex up as Munchkins and taught them the song and dance. In his eyes I could do no wrong. It was a terrible responsibility and I worried all the time about letting him down.

He was only six years old. I thought back to when I was six and remembered feeling the same way toward Janna that he did toward me. Had she worried about letting me down or doing something that might turn me against her?

Maybe she did. And maybe that was why she'd taken so much sass from me this past year without telling me to go jump in the lake. At the same time, though, I knew that if Danny had started acting rotten to me, I probably would have put up with it, too, just as Janna had.

Being someone's idol was a pretty tough job. I could see that now. How had Janna managed to carry me on her back all those years without rebelling? On the other hand, would I rebel if I had Danny looking up to me for years and years? No. No, I would think I was very lucky to have someone like that in my life.

After the party, I'd stopped wearing wigs. I'd begun wearing a kerchief wrapped buccaneer style around my head, with huge hoop earrings.

Eliot said I looked like a Caribbean gris-gris.

"What's a gris-gris?" I asked.

"It's a voodoo woman. A female hoodoo."

Danny loved that. He loved calling me his "hoodoo." We even worked up a comedy routine.

"Yoo Hoo," I'd say.

"Are you a hoodoo?" he'd say.

"A what do?"

"A hoodoo."

"No. Do you do hoodoo?"

"If you do, I do," he'd answer, laughing help-lessly, even though we'd done this corny routine time after time.

Little kids are like that. If they think a joke is good the first time around, it's even better the twentieth. But something about Danny's laughter made me laugh too. Sometimes I'd laugh until tears came. And then I'd wonder if the tears were for him or for me.

I love Irish music. I'd brought a tape of Irish songs with me to Hope House, to play on my boom box. "Danny Boy" was on one of them.

I played it once for Danny. Never again.

He thought it was "pretty." I thought it was heartbreaking.

Even the melody of "Danny Boy" makes you want to lay your head on your arms and cry. The lyrics make you want to lie right down and die.

There's a last verse to the song that nearly fin-ished me off. In it, the singer asks that when Danny Boy returns at last to Ireland, and finds her dead and buried, he visit her grave and say a prayer for her over it.

The idea of a grave—Danny's or mine—was too much for me. You can only accept so much and then no more.

Maybe there was something prophetic in that song, something I'd always known would happen. Maybe that was why the song made me want to cry. Maybe memories run forward as well as backward. And maybe I'd always known I was fated to love a little boy named Danny, and that he would die.

I should have guessed that Danny wasn't feeling well. He'd grown so tired. He'd been up too late the night before, I told myself. He'd done too much.

His parents looked anxious. They visited every day. His mother was lovely, just as I'd known Danny's mother would be. Her heart was in her eyes, those same lovely, large brown eyes as Danny's. To lose Danny would be to lose everything—her life, her happiness, her future.

Still, I told myself that Danny was fine. I refused to discuss the possibility of his dying with Eliot. I was like granite. I told him that Danny would live longer than any of us. I denied the future up one side and down the other.

They took Danny to St. Stephen's in the middle of the night.

We weren't allowed to visit him the next day. He was in the Isolation Unit.

And still I denied that he would die. They would do chemotherapy on him. They would use experimental drugs. He would go into remission.

Danny died. It was on a Monday morning they told us.

I went into such a terrible depression that it

affected the way I saw colors. I literally saw everything in shades of gray. It was as if a terrible pall hung between me and the rest of the world.

I cried for Danny. There was so much to cry about. There were so many things that Danny, now, would never know. He would never grow up. He would never become a man. He would never have children and do all the things that most people take for granted.

I cried and cried. I couldn't stop crying for Danny.

Dr. Graham came. He gave me a shot of something.

And then I had a funny dream. It must have been the effect of the shot. I felt as if I were looking through the large end of a telescope. Instead of things being bigger, they were smaller. Everything I looked at was small. Unimportant, even. Far away. Nothing seemed to matter.

The secret of living—what was important and what was not—was made clear to me then, instantly, briefly. Being happy seemed such an easy thing. It was merely a matter of the will. You willed yourself happiness and it came. I wish now I could remember the how and why of it and the feeling of seeing life as it must look from the far side of eternity. It was so simple at the time.

"Beth! Beth!" said a voice, calling me back to life.

I awoke. It was another day and Eliot was sitting by my bed.

"Beth," he said. "Wake up. I have good news. The doctors say I won't lose my leg after all!"

11

The sun was shining. Little dust motes danced in a beam that shone through the window. Eliot was sitting in my bedside chair. His face was alight. His blue eyes blazed with happiness.

"I'm not going to lose my leg after all, Beth!" he said. Then he repeated it, for the pure joy of hearing the words as they fell again from his lips. "I'm not going to lose my leg!"

Am I still asleep? I wondered. Is this a part of that secret of happiness dream?

I struggled to an upright position. No, this was no dream. The room spun briefly and then righted itself. That must have been some shot Dr. Graham gave me.

I shook my head to clear the fog from my brain. "Eliot! Your leg? Oh Eliot, Eliot, I'm so happy! When did you find out?"

"Just now. This morning. You've been conked

out, dead to the world. Snoring, even. But I had to wake you up. I couldn't wait."

"I'm so glad you did. Didn't. Did wake me up. Didn't wait!" I was so excited and happy I didn't know whether to laugh or cry. "This is like a wonderful dream. I can hardly believe it, it's so wonderful!"

"Yes! *Yes!* YES!" As if he couldn't bear to sit still a moment longer, Eliot jumped from his chair, grasped the top of the door frame and did a couple of quick pull-ups.

"I'm going to have two legs, Beth, just like everyone else!" he shouted joyfully. "It's the greatest thing that's ever happened to me. I'll be able to walk and jog and dance. I'm going to learn all those fancy ballroom dances, too, so you and I can be a team, like Fred and Ginger. Would you like that, Beth?"

He lowered himself to the floor and sat down again beside me. "You do dance, don't you, Beth?"

I nodded, my face quivering. I couldn't speak. If I did, I might burst into tears.

He squeezed my hand. "Well, actually, I'm probably getting a little carried away. I might not be able to jog. And I might have to limit my dancing to a slow two-step. That leg bone is kind of fragile. The radiation has weakened it to the point that it could break very easily. But what the heck!

At least I have something there beneath my knee. Something to stand on and walk with. And I can always wear a leg brace if the doctors think I need it."

I dashed a hand across my eyes and gave a wobbly smile.

"Can you bicycle across the United States in a leg brace?" I managed to say.

"Sure. Sure I can. Listen, Beth, I read about this guy who bicycled across the United States with an artificial leg. So I ought to be able to do it with a brace."

His eyes narrowed thoughtfully. "As a matter of fact, after I do the United States, there's something else I want to do.

"Oh no," I moaned. "What now?"

"I want to bicycle across the Sahara."

"The Sahara? The Sahara *desert*? How can you possibly bicycle across a desert?"

"There's a road, of course. I read about it in the *National Geographic*."

"Well, if you think I'm going to come along behind on a camel with the supplies, forget it," I said. "That desert sun is murder on a girl's complexion."

We laughed together comfortably, joyfully.

And then, like a cold hand laid suddenly upon my heart came the thought, *Danny's dead. We're*

laughing—how can we laugh—and Danny is dead.
Dead. Forever and ever dead.

"Danny," I said. "Danny's dead."

"Yes."

"And here we are, laughing and talking, just as if everything's okay."

"No we aren't. We're happy because I'm not going to lose my leg."

Eliot waited for that to sink in and then said, "Danny's dead and there's nothing we can do about it, Beth. You can wear black and not smile all the rest of your life, but it isn't going to bring him back."

"I know that, Eliot, but it just doesn't seem right, somehow, to go on as if nothing's happened."

"We aren't going on as if nothing's happened. Something *has* happened. Something terrible. But we *are* going on. We have to."

He looked around the room desperately, as if he hoped to see something written on the wall, something wise that he could quote to me.

"Look, Beth," he finally said. "Life has certain rules. And the biggest one is that you go on, no matter what. If the world stopped turning around because a loved one died, it would still be sitting like a dead rock in space while we all mourned the deaths of Adam and Eve."

What he said was almost laughable, but it made sense in a peculiar sort of way.

"But he was so little, Eliot. He was only six years old."

"We all have to die sometime," Eliot said. "Some people just do it faster than others. The important thing is not how *long* you live, but how *much*, and how *well*. Danny brought a lot of joy into the world, didn't he?"

I nodded tearfully.

"And he brought a lot of love, too, didn't he?"

I nodded again.

"Then maybe that was a successful life, and he didn't have to live any longer to do what he was supposed to do."

It was a comforting way of looking at it, and I was grateful to Eliot for pointing it out to me. The thought that little Danny accomplished in six short years what most people took decades and decades to do made me feel better. I knew, though, that I would never—for as long as I lived —be able to listen to that song, "Danny Boy," or see *The Wizard of Oz*, or even smell a lollipop again without a sick sense of loss, that black feeling of loneliness for a little boy I'd loved briefly but with all my heart.

Then another thought hit me.

"Oh Eliot," I gasped. "You went through tests on your leg and you didn't tell anyone about it."

"I didn't want to. Everyone was all torn up about Danny. I thought I'd wait and see how things turned out."

I reached over to my nightstand and drew a Kleenex from the box. I blew my nose heartily with lots of sound effects. Then I slam dunked the wadded up Kleenex into my wastebasket.

"How come you're so smart, Eliot? How come you know all the right things to say? Were you a saint or something in a previous incarnation?"

Eliot laughed. "Hardly. It's just that I've had cancer longer than you have. It's a great teacher."

I blew my nose again on a fresh Kleenex. "Listen, Eliot, all things considered, you're really something. I know this is kind of sudden, but when we're old enough, will you marry me?"

"Are you telling me your intentions are strictly honorable?" he asked in mock amazement. "You mean, you haven't been trifling with my affections all this time?"

"Yes, I have," I said, shaking my head regretfully. "But now I see the error of my ways. You are a jewel, Eliot. A veritable ruby."

I paused for dramatic effect. "And the truth of the matter is, I want to make an honest man of you."

Eliot pretended to think it over.

"Okay, Beth, I'll marry you. I've seen you mean

and mad and bald and bawling, not to mention throwing up rather swinishly, but I do love you in spite of everything.''

I gawked up at him, jaw agape. I'd been talking utter nonsense. He sounded serious.

He leaned over toward me. ''Close your mouth, Beth,'' he commanded. I did.

Then he kissed me. He'd never done that before. No boy ever had. His lips were warm and firm and his breath was spicy, like ginger cookies.

I liked it—the kiss and the idea that he loved me, that my darling Eliot loved me.

I liked it very much.

''There,'' he said. ''That ought to show you I mean business.''

Danny was buried two days later.

Mom said she couldn't go, that it would destroy her to see a man and woman burying their six-year-old child.

Surprisingly, Janna said she would take me. When she told me that, I saw a flash of the old Janna, that fierce, protective look she used to get when I was little and she felt I needed someone to look out for me.

Eliot and Rachel came with us. Danny's dying had hurt Rachel too. She'd been fond of him, as everyone at Hope House had, and when the news of his death came, she'd had a relapse. All the progress she'd made fighting her anorexia seemed to go right out the window. She refused to eat, and Nurse McGehan found her in the bathroom, trying to make herself throw up.

Ms. McGehan took her out to the garden, where they walked up and down for a long time on the paths between the rose bushes. I don't know what she said to Rachel—Rachel would never say—but it seemed to help.

Janna looked very grown-up and sophisticated when she came to drive us to the burial. Her hair was pulled back and knotted in a bun. She wore a severely cut navy blue suit. Her eyes were hidden behind huge, wraparound sunglasses.

I knew why she'd worn them. She was afraid she'd cry and didn't want me to see, for fear it might set me off again.

I didn't feel like crying though. Maybe you have only so many tears to shed for each sorrow in your life, and I'd already spent the share allotted me for Danny.

But I did have a hard, tight lump in my chest. It was like a rock, a rock that would not dissolve, and I'd resigned myself to the belief I would have it in there forever.

Danny's little casket seemed so small, and the hole dug for it was so deep. Baskets of flowers stood all around the grave, three deep in some places. Danny would have liked that, I thought. Danny loved flowers so.

The minister stood beside the open grave and talked. My mind wandered a bit as he said his few, final words about death and Danny and loss and remembering. I'd already thought all that through a hundred times.

But then the minister ended with a quote that was so meaningful to me and so beautiful that I bolted up on my folding chair and felt my heart expand in my chest and that hard little lump melt and flow away.

He was saying, "*. . . love will have been enough. There is a land of the living and a land of the dead and the bridge is love, the only survival, the only meaning.*"

I found out later the quotation was from a famous book. Janna told me. But at that moment, I could see the bridge—see it as clearly as if it were in front of me—that bridge of love, stretching in a rainbow arc between two worlds, the world of the living and the world of the dead.

The quote was from *The Bridge of San Luis Rey* by Thornton Wilder, Janna said when we were alone in my room.

"I have the book at home," she said. "I had to read it for English lit last year and fell in love with it. I read it whenever I'm feeling down."

She brought me the book the following day. She'd made a special trip just to bring it to me. I kissed her when we parted, and she held me close for a moment before she ran off down the stairs. I loved her then, as I used to love her. She was my Janna, my sister. There was no one like her anywhere.

"Janna!" I called after her.

She paused in her flight and turned. "What, Bethie?"

"I . . . I just want to thank you for being my sister."

She didn't reply. Just blew me a kiss.

It was a small, thin volume. I read it very quickly. As I closed it, after that final, powerful paragraph, I knew why Janna had brought it to me. She'd found an answer in that book. Not an answer, exactly. Rather, a conclusion. An understanding. And she hoped I would too.

The story takes place long, long ago in Peru. A bridge over the Andes breaks and five people fall to their deaths. A priest, who witnesses the accident, wonders *why*. Why were these particular people marked for death.

He makes a study of their lives. He takes pages and pages of notes in the hope he might find out what it was, what they all had in common, that caused them to die in such a sudden and terrible way. He finds there is no answer. That's it. There is no answer, the author tells us.

But then, like Hope flying out of Pandora's box after Trouble has escaped, he says that the only concrete thing we have to hang on to as we fumble our way through life is love. Love is what ties the past to the future and gives us the hope we need to survive. Love, the bridge, the only meaning to the puzzle of life.

Dr. Graham has said many times that "why?" is the question everyone asks when they find they have cancer. "Why? What have I done to deserve this? Is this some kind of punishment? Why me? Why? Why? Why?"

After that afternoon, after Danny's funeral, I stopped asking, "Why me?"

I knew the answer.

Or rather, I knew that there was no answer.

12

I went back into St. Stephen's Hospital for more chemotherapy only a couple of days after Danny's funeral.

I hadn't been feeling very well, and my blood tests weren't good, so my oncologist, Dr. Lindberg, talked to Dr. Gordon, who'd been monitoring my progress at Hope House. They decided I'd better get started on my second-line chemotherapy right away. They hoped they could induce a complete remission this time.

The kids at Hope House were pretty low-key about saying good-bye and wishing me a quick recovery and all the usual things that people say and do when you're about to go into a hospital. The truth is, they were superstitious. They'd learned to be superstitious about things like that. They'd learned not to count on someone returning from the hospital cured. Or even returning. Danny hadn't, and that was the first thing everyone thought about when I said I had to go in for more chemo.

A lot of people are superstitious. Actors are. They say, "Break a leg," instead of "Good luck" on opening night. They don't allow whistling in a dressing room, and believe that a hat on the bed means someone's going to die.

Well, we Hope House kids had a few superstitions too. Our version of "break a leg" was to give the person going back into the hospital a bunch of yucky things like bedpans and spit basins and bathroom deodorant sprays. And someone, I don't know who it was or when it started, got everybody afraid to hang anything from a bedpost or a doorknob for fear of bringing bad luck. Maybe whoever it was had been remembering bed charts and IVs and nurses' call buttons—things that hang and drape around a hospital room—and didn't want anything to remind him or her of it.

And no one ever, *ever*, laid a hat on a bed in Hope House.

A bunch of the kids got together at Hope House the night before I went back into the hospital. They were careful not to call it a good-bye party, although that's what it was. They pretended they'd just all decided to get together in my honor.

We didn't do much, just kind of hung out together in the living room and popped corn and toasted marshmallows in the fireplace.

I opened the presents they'd given me. Eliot had gone to a joke store and bought a Halloween fright wig—one of those things that stick out in all directions. I put it on and modeled it.

"You look like you just jammed your finger in a light socket," Lydia said. "You could at least have made Beth a blonde while you were at it, Eliot. I hear they have more fun."

"And gentlemen prefer them," said Rachel sourly. "Why, I cannot possibly imagine."

"But gentlemen marry brunets," Steve put in. "So don't give up hope, Rachel. There's a man out there for you. Somewhere. Maybe. If you're lucky."

"Sexist pig," said Lydia.

Steve threw up his hands. "I was only trying to give the poor girl something to live for."

"For your information, Mr. Smarty Pants Sit-Down Comic," Rachel retorted, "it just so happens that catching a man is *not* number one on my wish list right now."

"I love a fiery, hot-tempered woman," Steve said.

He wheeled himself over to where Rachel sat and leaned forward until he was eyeball-to-eyeball with her. "Look deep into my eyes and surrender yourself to me. You are feeling drowsy, very drowsy . . .''

"Help, Lydia!" Rachel squealed. "Make him go away. You started all this."

Lydia jumped up and wheeled Steve into a corner.

"You are sooo bad, Steve," she scolded. "You can stay here until you're ready to act like a gentleman."

"I could be here forever," Steve moaned.

Steve's present was a bunch of brown lunch bags, tied with a bright red ribbon.

"They are to be used," he said, "for barfing."

He'd written a joke on each one. "These are original Stevie Spencer jokes," he said. "I thought them up myself. Just think, Beth, when I'm famous and doing my sit-down comedy act in Las Vegas, you can tell people you were the first, the very first, to barf at them."

There were other presents, too, funny ones yet thoughtful. I realized then how much the kids at Hope House meant to me, and how it had helped me these past few weeks just having them around to talk to and cry with.

We'd all drawn closer to each other after the Celebrity Party. That was the thing that seemed to break down all the walls between us. And then, of course, being sick and not having to "put on" in front of each other or worry about our looks and popularity did the rest. We'd seen each other, warts and all, as the saying goes, and what we felt now for each other was an unconditional friendship.

Unconditional friendships are hard to find. I'd never had one before. I mean, when you're little, you're always saying things like, "You can't be my friend unless you . . ." Or, "You're not my friend because you . . ." Or, "I'll be your friend if you . . ."

Conditional words, *unless*, *because*, *if*. As you grow older, you don't say it straight out anymore, but it's there, under the surface.

But now I'd begun to realize you can't put conditions and limitations on friendship. You had to accept people for what they were. Maybe it was because I was in a lifeboat now, that lifeboat Eliot told me about, and I needed friends as I never had before. I needed someone to help me paddle. To help me survive.

I even needed Rachel, my roommate. Rachel, who'd put the white chalk mark down the middle of our room to keep me from messing up her side.

I could laugh at that chalk mark now, even though I knew Rachel was still a first-class pain in the neck with her pickiness. But I didn't mind that anymore. I saw beyond her prissy, neat little surface to her inner self which was caring and loving and anxious to please.

Rachel had become like family to me, and you know how it is with family. You have to love them even if you don't like their habits. You have no choice.

After I'd opened my presents, we all sat there in front of the fireplace, watching the logs shift and pop and the fire die. It was a comfortable time, and I remember thinking, "I'll remember this always. This moment, these people."

No one said anything about Danny. We weren't ready for that, yet. In the meantime, though, there were a lot of happy things to talk about.

Lydia said she was sure Dr. Graham and Dr. Ambrose's romance was turning into "the real thing."

"They're dating all the time now, and my mother saw them in this real fancy restaurant, holding hands and looking absolutely soppy about each other."

We were all happy for them. The thought that Dr. Graham, who'd been widowed ten years earlier, had found love and happiness again was especially meaningful for me. It proved what Eliot had tried to tell me, that the world does keep on turning after a tragedy.

Another piece of good news was that Carrie had been fitted for her new leg and was going to physical therapy to learn to walk on it.

"I'm doing real well," she told us. "It's amazing how lifelike it is."

And Steve told us that he'd been scheduled to do a comedy act at assembly when he went back to school.

"I'll be famous," he said. "All the hot chicks will be fighting over me."

"Oh, good grief!" said Rachel.

"But naturally I'm not interested. I'm waiting for you, Rachel. When you lose all that baby fat, that is."

Rachel punched him in the shoulder but she looked secretly pleased.

Eliot and I had a little quiet time together after everyone else had gone up to bed.

"How is it we always wind up the last at the party?" I asked.

"I think they were being tactful," Eliot replied. "They know we'd like a little time alone to talk."

And how we talked! We talked about the future. We talked, without saying so exactly, as if we might be sharing it, he and I. Maybe we were just being young and dumb, but it was nice to think of having Eliot in my life for years to come, and he seemed to feel the same way about me.

The only problem was that the unspoken word "if" lurked beneath the surface of everything we said. We might talk about what we planned to do when we graduated from college, but we each silently thought, "*If* I graduate from college. *If* I'm healthy when I'm twenty-one. *If* my cancer hasn't come back."

"So tomorrow's the big day," Eliot said. "Are you all packed up for the hospital?"

"Yes, and I'm counting on going into a complete remission this time. They're using some new drugs. New for me, anyway. I've always been healthy. If they work on anyone, they ought to work on me."

I sounded confident, but I was afraid. I worried about what would happen if it didn't put me into remission. I had a funny, cold feeling in the pit of my stomach and my ESP, like a phonograph needle on a broken record, kept repeating Murphy's Law: "If something can possibly go wrong, it will."

I didn't tell Eliot this, though. I tried to sound as cheerful and optimistic as I could. Ever since we'd met, I'd been leaning on him and taking from him. It was time, I thought, to stop freeloading off him. It was time to be as courageous and full of hope as he was.

"I'm thinking positively," I told him, lying through my teeth. I repeated myself once more, just for good measure. "Yes, I'm thinking positively about this chemo."

"Good, and I'll be waiting for you when you get

out of the hospital," Eliot said. "And if they allow me to visit you, I'll sit there and hold your hand when you get sick."

"Maybe I won't get as sick this time as last," I said hopefully. "And maybe this course of treatment won't be as long as before."

My ESP was wrong. Murphy's Law did not apply to my chemotherapy.

Five weeks later I was in a state of complete remission. Dr. Lindberg threw everything at me but the kitchen sink, he said, my body was that resistant to standard therapy. But he *did* get me into remission.

That was the good news.

And then he told me he had me scheduled for a bone marrow transplant.

13

"But why?" I asked. "You just said I was in a complete remission, didn't you?"

Dr. Lindberg stood at the foot of my bed. Mom, Dad, and Janna were perched anxiously on ringside chairs. Obviously they knew all about the doctor's decision to give the go-ahead on the bone marrow transplant.

"Why?" I asked again. There was a whine in my voice. "If I'm in a complete remission, why can't I go home now and start living a normal life again?"

Dr. Lindberg might look like a Viking with his blue eyes and red-gold mustache, but right now he was acting more like an old-time Mississippi gambler. That was some joker he'd just pulled from his cuff, and I told him so.

Dr. Lindberg knotted his long, slender fingers together. I heard the pop of a small bone. I could tell he was trying to find the right words to explain his decision to me.

"Look, Beth," he began, "every leukemia case is unique and must be treated specifically."

"Well, I certainly know *that*, Doctor."

My whine had turned into a harumph.

"Your leukemia has proven resistant to standard therapy, and I'm afraid your remission might not last—that you might go into a relapse."

He paused for a moment and let that sink in before continuing.

"Bone marrow transplants are primarily used on patients whose malignancies, like yours, are resistant to therapy. Used with a high rate of success, I might add. Do you follow me so far?"

I nodded. "But why didn't you tell me?"

"Because, first of all, I had to get you into a state of complete remission. Success with the transplant is more likely when the patient is in a complete remission. I wasn't sure what the results of this last course of chemo would be, and your family and I thought you had enough to worry about at the time without adding to it."

I glanced over at Mom and Dad. They both looked older and thinner than they had when this all started. And tired. Very, very tired.

"The second reason I didn't tell you," continued Dr. Lindberg, "was because I had to find the right bone marrow donor, the perfect genetic match. We were lucky. Janna tested out. She's going to be your donor."

Janna spoke up. "I kept telling the doctor all along that I was the one, Beth. Of course I'm the perfect donor for you. After all, you're my little sister. We're almost a part of each other."

She rose from her chair and came over to my bed, laying a warm, firm hand on my shoulder.

The evasive, denying Janna that I'd been seeing over the past few weeks was gone. In its place was the old Janna, the Janna I'd known all my life. The Janna who was proud and protective of me and willing to take on anyone and anything to prove it.

Now that Janna could actually *do* something to help me, I realized, she stopped avoiding the fact that I was sick. It was the terrible feeling of helplessness that made her unable to face what I was up against.

How I loved her at that moment. I knew then that I had always loved Janna, even when I thought I didn't, and that I always would. We were sisters, and sisterhood is a special bond that can never be broken. We shared so much—blood, family, background, experiences. I knew I would never share that particular uniqueness with anyone else. And I knew that, even if I lived to be a hundred, I could never pay her back for what she was prepared to do for me at that moment. I also knew that I would spend what was left of my life doing the right thing by Janna, just as she had always done right by me.

I looked up at her and bit my lips to keep them from quivering.

"Oh Janna," I managed to say. My voice sounded teary and high-pitched. "Aren't you getting tired of rushing to my rescue all the time?"

She laughed and hugged me. "Believe me, I'm going to collect for this one, Beth. Dr. Lindberg says that for a few days after they remove my absolutely perfect, flawlessly healthy bone marrow and give it to you, I'm going to feel as if I've been kicked in the hip by a horse. I wouldn't do that for just anybody, you know. . . ."

Before he left us, Dr. Lindberg explained the transplantation procedure to us. He began by cautioning us that there were no guarantees and that sometimes the cancer patient's body rejects the donated bone marrow.

"Not this time," Janna said. She wasn't joking or trying to sound optimistic. I could tell she meant it. Her chin stuck out resolutely. "Not this time. I know just as sure as I'm standing here that it will take. I know it!"

Then the doctor told us what would happen next: that I'd rest up a couple of weeks in the hospital before I started on the transplant chemo.

The transplant chemo, he said, would be rough because they'd be using high doses of radiation and chemotherapy to completely turn off my immune system so it wouldn't reject the transplant, and to kill off any hidden malignant cancer cells. They would give me medication, though, that would make me sleep through most of it.

"Many transplant patients can't remember this period later," he said. "It's almost as if they've had a temporary amnesia."

The actual transplant procedure, he told us, was quite simple. Janna would be anesthetized and a quantity of bone marrow would be removed from her hip bone. Then it would be injected into me, like a blood transfusion.

Then, if all went well, in two to three weeks it would manufacture a new supply of healthy, cancer-free blood cells for my body.

"And it *will* work. It will!" Janna said, clenching her fists.

There was something I had to tell her. Something important.

"Listen, Janna," I said earnestly. "If it shouldn't work, if my body rejects the marrow or something, promise me you won't think it's your fault. It won't be, you know, any more than it's my fault for having leukemia. It will just be one of those things and we'll go on from there."

"I refuse to listen to this silly, defeatist talk,"

Janna said in the strict, severe tones she used on me when I was little and she was forbidding me to pick my nose or scratch my bottom in public. "It's going to work, Beth, and that's all there is to it!"

Dr. Lindberg made me stay in semi-isolation while I rested up from the chemo that had put me into remission.

At first he felt I shouldn't have any visitors, aside from my family. He said he didn't want me to catch any germs prior to the transplant. But then he relented.

"I guess your mental health should count for something," he said. "Okay, Beth, you can see your friends from Hope House, providing they wear masks, gloves, and gowns."

That would be easy for them. They were used to that.

Eliot, of course, came every day. His mouth was covered by a mask, but I didn't need to see it. I could see his smile in his eyes.

"Well, you're coming down the homestretch now, Beth," he said.

"I'm trying to think of it as An Experience," I told him. "The last two words are capitalized."

Eliot's blue eyes looked puzzled.

"My mother," I explained. "That's what she always says. Whenever something unpleasant happens to her, she calls it An Experience. She has this theory that life is like a novel, and unless we have Experiences, capital 'E,' it's pretty dull reading. Not," I amended hastily, "that she ever figured on leukemia as an acceptable experience."

Eliot would be at Hope House only for another week while his medical record and coming treatments were being reevaluated. His future, like mine, would always be a question mark, but during those lazy, golden hospital afternoons while I awaited my transplant, we made a pact that we would enjoy life as much as we could, and live it as well and as thoroughly as we were able.

In the meantime, we made plans to see each other when I returned home after the transplant. Eliot lived only a few miles from me, we'd discovered, and as he would be getting his driver's license when he turned sixteen, getting together would be no problem.

I'd never been out on a date—a real date—before, and I was glad that, when I did, it would be with Eliot. I was also glad that Eliot was the boy who'd given me my first kiss. I was collecting memories the way a miser collects gold coins, and I wanted only the most precious ones for my treasury.

The kids from Hope House came to visit. They brought funny balloons and cartoon cards and joke gifts. Anything to cheer me up and make me laugh.

Steve said most of the kids were getting ready to leave Hope House.

"Yeah, school bells are breaking up that old gang of mine," he said. "I'm back at school, too, and my comedy routine is booked for next Tuesday."

Carrie raised her eyebrows. "And heaven help the Student Body when old cornball here starts on one of his routines."

"He'll knock them dead, that's what he'll do," Rachel said, smiling at Steve, who blushed furiously.

There was definitely something going on between those two.

Carrie was now wearing her new artificial leg. She was getting around on it quite well. She still wore slacks over it, but I figured one of these days she'd break loose and wear a skirt.

"I'm even starting to put on weight, have you noticed?" Rachel asked, patting a skeletal hip. "I had my first hot fudge sundae in ages yesterday. That ought to mean something."

"It means you're turning into a real dishy number, that's what it means," Steve said.

This time it was Rachel's turn to blush.

"Steve's right. The old gang will be breaking up

soon, that's for sure,'' Lydia said. ''It's sad, but everyone's ready to get back to real life.''

The thought of everyone splitting up and going in different directions was a bleak one, but we all knew we'd be seeing each other as outpatients at Hope House and we solemnly promised each other we'd hold regular reunions. Somehow I had the feeling everyone would follow through on that promise. At least for a while. And if we all got so caught up again in normal, happy lives, to the point that our old relationships at Hope House were no longer important, then hurray for that! After all, wasn't that what we all wanted for each other?

I cherished the visits from my friends, but more than that, even, I cherished the alone time I had in the hospital.

I had a television and a radio, but I rarely played them. I liked the silence. I needed it. I felt like one of those old hermit saints who used to go out to the desert and live in caves. There are times in your life when you need to be alone, just to think.

My room was on a high floor at St. Stephen's. I would sit in a leather armchair by the window and look down at the world.

I tried to recapture the dream I'd had after Danny died, when Dr. Graham had given me the shot to make me sleep. When I could see what was important and what was not, and being happy seemed such an easy thing.

When I looked down from my hospital window, everyone looked so small. People were small. Cars were small. Everyone seemed to be scurrying around, like busy little ants.

When I was little I had one of those ant farms you buy in pet stores. Funny, I'd almost forgotten about it. Anyway, Janna helped me set up the ant farm with the sand and gravel and the special little ants that come with it, and I watched them eagerly, every chance I got, to see what they would do.

I got real excited when they rushed around and moved some crushed white gravel from one side of the container to the other and built little tunnels through it.

Oboy, I thought. Something important's going to come of this!

And then those stupid ants scurried around and moved it all back again, and I realized with a great sense of disenchantment that ants aren't industrious. They're just plain dumb! And what's more, they're workaholics. And for what? To move gravel from one side of a jar and then back again, that's what!

I thought about those ants as I looked down from my window.

I wondered how many of those people down

there were like the ants in my old ant farm. How many were rushing around, moving gravel from one side of a jar to the other and then back again for no good reason?

If I'd learned anything from having leukemia, and Dr. Graham told me that learning was a part of the experience of cancer, then I'd learned that our time here on earth is precious because it doesn't last very long. And the strength of our bodies is precious because it can be taken away at any moment. And our efforts are important, because they have to have meaning.

If I lived to adulthood, I told myself, I wouldn't be like one of those silly ants. I wouldn't rush around endlessly, frantically busy but doing nothing of consequence. No, I vowed, I'd try to do something meaningful with my life. Something important.

Then I had to stop and smile at myself. Isn't this what most people do when they think they haven't long to live? Make promises to do wonderful things if they're allowed to live?

Yes, I answered myself. But maybe a lot of people *do* live up to their vows. And maybe I would too. Yes. Yes, I would.

14

So here we are at last. All these past weeks have been pointing us toward today.

Tomorrow they start me on what I call my "killer countdown chemo" to prepare my body for the bone marrow transplant.

Dr. Lindberg has just left. Mom, Dad, Janna, and I are sitting here, talking.

We've come a long way, all of us, individually and as a group, from that first terrible night when Mom laid her head down on the sink and bawled, and Dad didn't know how to comfort her. The fear and the weeping, the denying and the pretending are gone now.

I remember what Dr. Graham told us: "An experience as traumatic as cancer affects the entire family. No family member will go through this unchanged. My goal is to see that the change is for the better."

Well, here's to you, Dr. Graham. As they say, you done real good.

It's impossible to actually see bonds between family members, of course, but you can feel them. I feel ours are stronger now than they've ever been before. Mom and Dad's chairs are set close together and my parents seem to touch each other more now than they used to. Nothing romantic actually, just little things, like Mom touching Dad's sleeve when she says something that's directed to him alone, or Dad patting her hand supportively when we talk about the future.

Janna is sitting by my side at the head of the bed. She used to sit like this when I was little and in bed with a cold. In those days, she used to tell me stories. Now there are no stories, only straight talk.

We discuss the possibility that the bone marrow transplant might not work, and what we will do if it doesn't.

"First of all, I'm confident it *will* work," Dad says. "But if it doesn't, and Beth should have another relapse, then we go for more chemotherapy. Look—the treatment of cancer is advancing by leaps and bounds. They're discovering new drugs, new treatments, even as we speak. Who knows what new cure will be discovered in the near future?"

Janna shifts restlessly in the chair beside me.

"This conversation is purely academic," she says. "Beth's body will *not* reject my bone marrow."

She raises her hand as if to fend off any further argument. "I know this transplant's going to work. Don't ask me how I know, I just know, that's all. Haven't my premonitions always turned out right? Doesn't everybody say I have Grandmother Farrell's Irish gift of The Sight?"

She pauses and glares around at all of us.

"So that's it. Amen. End of discussion."

We all laugh a little and relax at that. Janna's Irish ESP has always been a household word.

"I think we should take a family holiday afterward," Mom says. "We haven't had a vacation in a long time. What do you think, George?"

"Good idea," Dad says. "How about something . . . restful?"

"Forget it," I say. "Not camping. I refuse to go camping!"

"And I'm not going to Disneyland," Mom puts in. "No Mickey Mouse—please. I'm not interested."

"So what do you think, Janna?" Dad asks.

Janna looks off, dreamy-eyed. "Water," she says. "Something on the water. Some place where we can lie on the sand and soak up the sun."

"Bermuda," Dad says. "Or the Bahamas.

Would you like that, Beth? Would you like the Bahamas?"

He's looking at me intently, pleadingly. Suddenly his eyes fill with tears. They spill over, like a flash flood, and run down his cheeks.

"Bethie," he says. The sorrow of a lifetime is in his voice. "Bethie, my sweet baby girl."

We're all crying now. Not just a teary crying, but a sobbing, gusty crying. Everyone is in everyone else's arms.

I'm the first to recover. I sit up and blow my nose.

"There's something I want you all to know," I say. "Something I want you to remember, no matter what happens."

They are all looking at me now.

"I'm not afraid anymore," I tell them. "I'm ready to accept whatever comes."

And then I find myself quoting Eliot's words to them:

"We all have to die sometime," I say. "Some people just do it faster than others, that's all. The important thing is not how long you live, but how much and how well. . . ."

Janna lingers behind after Mom and Dad have gone.

"I have something for you, Beth," she says.

She pulls something from her jacket pocket. It's

a small, cut-crystal star on a silver chain. Her fingers tremble slightly as she hangs it on my bedpost.

"Uncle Ed once said I had Star Quality," she says, "but he was wrong. You're the one with Star Quality. You've always had it, but haven't used it until now."

I blink back my tears and struggle to get my voice under control before answering her.

"But you *do* have Star Quality, Janna," I tell her. "And it doesn't matter if I don't have it now because I soon will."

I reach over and take my sister's hand.

"Because," I say, "when I leave this hospital, there's going to be a little bit of you in me."

Here is a preview of the third book in the Day by Day series, *Dying to Eat*, coming in September.

Food Intake, November 8

Breakfast
    one 8-oz. glass skim milk
    one bowl shredded wheat with skim milk
    one orange
    one multivitamin

A.M. snack
    carrot sticks and apple slices

Lunch
    One high-protein milk shake
    one-half cup broccoli and cauliflower medley

Dinner
    one each: Snickers Bar, Almond Joy, Butterfinger, and Reese's Peanut Butter Cup. One entire chocolate cheesecake. One box Ding Dongs. One pint rocky road ice cream. One pint mint chocolate chip ice cream. One pint double-dark chocolate ice cream. And for dessert: one large bag of Hershey's Kisses.

finance the building of a new church for Saint Peter in Rome. Buying an indulgence was a commercial transaction; it was like buying a ticket to heaven, and it was advertised as such. However grave a person's sin may have been, it was immediately forgiven the moment he bought this indulgence. Even a person who was already dead and whose soul was thought to be in purgatory could get to heaven if his offspring bought indulgences for him.

Johann Tetzel, a priest who was commissioned to sell indulgences, beguiled believers, playing on their sympathies for departed relatives and friends whom they might release from their sufferings in purgatory "as soon as the penny tinkles in the box." Thus, God's spiritual gift of salvation was corrupted into a commodity to be bought like a sack of wheat. In this manner the church of that day, like the church in Thyatira, became depraved.

In verses 21-23 Jesus said He would cast the church that did not repent of fornication into a bed and kill its children. Therefore, which church we choose to attend is a question of spiritual life or death.

Verse 21 reads, "I gave her space to repent." Several times Jesus gave opportunities for the church to repent in the dark period of the Middle Ages. Various movements arose and challenged the church to repent and reform.

One of the first was the Albigenses, which arose around 1170 in southern France. Rejecting the rites of the church, it put its effort into distributing copies of the New Testament. In those days the church forbade lay believers to read the Bible. Every local church had only one copy, and even that was chained to the pulpit so no one had access to it.

When this reform movement became strong, Pope Innocent III sent crusaders and annihilated the Albigenses.

Another opportunity for repentance came with the Waldense movement in 1170. Peter Waldo, a merchant of Lyon, France, was their leader. The Waldense disguised themselves as tradesmen and peddled wares, distributing copies of the New Testament and preaching the pure gospel as they traveled. However, this movement also came to a halt through persecution.

Yet another opportunity for repentance appeared with the reform movement led by John Wycliffe. An Englishman, he translated the Latin Bible into English and launched a campaign of spreading the Bible throughout the world.

Jan Hus, who was influenced by Wycliffe, became the rector of a university in Bohemia. He cried for reform in 1369, demanding that the church return to pure faith. In 1416 he was excommunicated by the pope and was finally burned to death in France.

On the day Hus was executed, the public square was filled with a large crowd. An effigy of a demon was bound to his body, which in turn was bound to a stake by a chain. Wood was heaped around his body up to his chin, then set on fire. Historians note that Hus sang hymns as the fire was ignited and began to burn his body. Numerous people witnessing the scene were moved to tears and became followers of the reform movement.

Another reform leader was Jerome Savonarola of Italy. He was filled with the Holy Spirit while praying. Whenever he preached in Florence, great crowds thronged the city. He also preached the restoration of a pure faith, shaking off the sacrificial rites. But like his predecessors, he was arrested, excommunicated and publicly executed.

Because the church refused to repent of her spiritual fornication, she had to be "cast...into a bed" (v. 22). That bed was the Protestant Reformation led by Martin Luther, which supplanted the Roman church as God's most faithful witness on earth.

V. To the Church in Sardis (3:1-6)

A. Destination

This letter was addressed to the church in Sardis, a city that flourished some five hundred years before John was born. Later the city was conquered by Cyrus of Persia, then by Alexander the Great. Through those conquests Sardis was reduced to ruins. In A.D. 17 a great earthquake turned the rebuilt city into a heap of refuse. However, Emperor Tiberius of Rome gave it new life. This city worshipped the goddess Cybele.

B. The Description of Jesus

Jesus appeared to the church in Sardis as One who had the seven Spirits of God and the seven stars. The seven stars signify the servants of God, and the seven Spirits of God signify that God gives the fullness of the Holy Spirit to the servants whom He has restored.

In the light of church history, the church in Sardis refers to the Protestant church founded by Luther on the biblical principle that we are justified by faith alone, not by good works and adherence to tradition.

C. Commendation

Jesus commended the few clothed in white robes in the church of Sardis. They were the ones who were justified before God by their faith, as were the leaders of the Reformation, who also retained pure faith. Because they believed in the precious blood of Jesus and His grace, He washed them clean and clothed them with white robes.

D. Rebuke

Jesus also rebuked the church in Sardis, saying, "Thou hast a name that thou livest, and art dead" (3:1). He meant that in the past the church had been growing and was alive, but little by little their enthusiasm disappeared and their faith became cold. Only a memory of the past was left.

Historically, the church of this period launched the Reformation, breaking with sacrifices and rituals of the Roman church. Since the reform was linked with many political motives, however, it was not completely changed.

E. Exhortation

Jesus exhorted the church in Sardis to be awakened to life from its dead state, to remember His graces received, to hold fast to the faith and repent.

F. Promise

Jesus promised that He would clothe with white robes those who were thus quickened to life and record their names in the book of life, that they might live forever (see v. 5). He would also vouch for those names before God and His angels.

G. Interpretation of the Prophecy (1517-1750)

In terms of church history, the church in Sardis signifies the period from 1517 to 1750. The name *Sardis* means "those escaping" — the people who left what became the Roman Catholic church. The most prominent figure of this period was Martin Luther, a priest who led the Reformation beginning in 1517. Through much fasting and prayer, he tried to obtain assurance of his salvation, but he was unable to do so. Therefore he was in agony.

On one occasion Luther visited Rome, where he ascended the steps of Pilate, the same stairs that tradition said Jesus had walked up to be tried before Pilate. Each step was strewn with pieces of broken glass, and pilgrims would go up on their knees to participate in the same sufferings as Jesus. Also, a superstition held that if people ascended the stairs on their knees, they would receive remission for their sins.

In the middle of climbing the stairs, Luther received a clear revelation from God: "The just shall live by faith" (Heb. 10:38). Hearing these words in his heart and suddenly realizing forgiveness comes not by deeds but by faith, he rose to his feet and descended the steps. It was considered sacrilegious to come down from the middle of those stairs, but Luther's heart was filled with the assurance of a firm biblical belief.

Returning from Rome, Luther posted a written protest of ninety-five articles on the church gate in Wittenberg, Germany, which firmly declared that indulgences were unbiblical. That written protest launched the Reformation, which freed the church from its dead state. Luther underwent numerous persecutions and was excommunicated, and his life was under constant threat. Fortunately, however, the king and the feudal lords of Germany protected him and saved his life. They had been struggling to free themselves from the rule of the pope and took advantage of the Reformation to revolt against Rome.

The result was that even though the Reformation was achieved, it had political as well as spiritual motives behind it. The church was still bound by form and ritual. And the church was actually still in the state of death, even though it had the appearance of being alive.

41

VI. To the Church in Philadelphia (3:7-13)

A. Destination

The destination of our Lord's sixth letter was to the believers in the church at Philadelphia. Located thirty miles southeast of Sardis, Philadelphia was also destroyed by the great earthquake of A.D. 17 and rebuilt by Tiberius. It was known for its wine, and drinking was a major problem.

B. The Description of Jesus

The Lord appeared to the church in Philadelphia as the One who had the key of David. When He opens, no one can shut, and when He shuts, no one can open. This signified that the Lord would cause a great revival in the Philadelphia church.

C. Commendation

Jesus commended the Philadelphian church for doing many activities with little ability and behaving sincerely, causing no shame to His name.

D. Rebuke

The Lord did not rebuke the Philadelphian church, a missionary church where a great revival took place (as it did in the church of Smyrna). He never rebukes a gospel-proclaiming, mission-sending church.

E. Exhortation

Jesus exhorted the Philadelphian church, which fulfilled its missionary role with little ability, to "hold that fast which thou hast" (v. 11). He didn't demand more than that but urged the church to preserve its enthusiasm for missions and service and to develop them more.

F. Promise

Jesus promised the Philadelphian church that if it kept the word of patience, continuing its mission work, He would keep it from the hour of temptation, when God will judge all the people who have lived on the earth.

To him who overcame, holding fast what he had, Jesus also gave the promise that He would make him a pillar in the temple (see v. 12). What does that mean? The pillar of the temple supports the house where God dwells. The blessed promise is that Jesus will make this church live forever with God.

Third, Jesus promised He would give the church a new name (see v. 12). Saying He would write the name of God, the name of New Jerusalem and His own new name means He would bless him who overcomes, that he may live forever in the New Jerusalem with the triune God.

G. Interpretation of the Prophecy
(1750-1905)

The church in Philadelphia foretold the church age between 1750 and 1905. *Philadelphia* means "brotherly love," and the church there preached the gospel with such love. Indeed, proclaiming the gospel is impossible unless we have compassion for our fellow men and women. When we do, Jesus opens the door of revival.

For a century and a half, from 1750 to 1905, churches experienced wonderful revival movements, and the fire spread to various parts of the world. A Society for China Inland Mission was formed in Great Britain, and through its efforts the gospel was preached to the inner parts of

China. The Student Volunteer Movement, also arising in Great Britain, became a great mission society.

Also during this period, the Methodist movement, the Salvation Army and the Holiness church arose. George Whitefield shook England, America and Europe with the gospel. Following him, numerous evangelical revivalists such as Jonathan Edwards, Charles Finney, Charles Spurgeon and Dwight Moody set America and Europe on fire.

As a result of the worldwide revival, a large number of missionaries went out inflamed with zeal. Leading figures among them were William Carey, who went to India; Robert Moffat, who went to Africa; and David Hill, who went to China. The revival and brisk mission activities continued until just before World War I.

Jesus' prophecy came true during the church age of Philadelphia. He also forewarned the church of the coming of great tribulation, but He promised He would cause the church to miss that tribulation.

VII. To the Church in Laodicea (3:14-22)

A. Destination

This letter was sent to Laodicea, forty miles north of Ephesus. In this city was a famous medical school, and eye salve made here became known for its healing power. Being a center of finance, Laodicea was extremely rich and one of the largest cities in Asia Minor.

Moreover, it was a city of entertainment, where all the citizens sought continual pleasure. Since the church had compromised with the world, it became neither cold nor hot.

B. The Description of Jesus

Jesus appeared to the church in Laodicea as One who was "the Amen, the faithful and true witness, the beginning of the creation of God" (v. 14). Accepting the Word of God with "amen" expresses our sincere loyalty to the Lord. Mankind was originally created that we might love God and give Him glory. Therefore when we bring glory to God by our faithful service, His original purpose for us is fulfilled.

The Laodicean church, however, had lost its loyalty to Christ, its true witness and the original purpose of creation. Jesus pointed out its hypocrisy and lifeless faith and urged it to repent.

C. Commendation

Among the six churches we have seen so far, no church failed to receive a commendation. However, the Laodicean church did not receive any commendation, only rebuke. It represents the church age in which we now live.

D. Rebuke

Jesus condemned the lukewarm faith of the Laodicean church: "So then because thou art lukewarm, and neither cold nor hot, I will spew thee out of my mouth" (v. 16).

Those are dreadful words. But I'm afraid many churches today have a Laodicean philosophy. Their people are either believers or unbelievers. They attend church when they want to and stay home when they don't They can accept the Bible as the Word of God or not. Sometimes the Scripture seems to have relevance to them, but sometimes not. Jesus hates the Laodicean church's lukewarm faith.

If faith is cold, Jesus can move a person toward repentance. On the other hand, people who vehemently oppose Jesus can easily be converted when their egos are crushed and they become hot with conviction. However, those people who go to church and give agreeable answers but whose hearts are not in it are the last kind to be converted.

Why was the church in Laodicea lukewarm in its faith? They had a wrong understanding of themselves. They said, "I am rich, and increased with goods, and have need of nothing" (v. 17). You can just imagine some of the leaders thinking, "The chapel building program is completed. Contributions continue to flow in. We're well-educated. Everything is so rich and fine. Therefore let's have fun in our faith life."

Today many American churches also allow their meetings to degenerate into social gatherings. On Sundays they have a short worship service, and then they enjoy eating and drinking under the false name of Christian fellowship.

"The kingdom of God is not meat and drink; but righteousness, and peace, and joy in the Holy Ghost" (Rom. 14:17). One time when I was in the United States conducting a crusade, I strongly rebuked some American churches for putting social activities ahead of God's work. They responded beautifully by sending money to poor Korean ministers.

While the Laodicean church thought itself rich, Jesus rebuked its spiritual poverty: "Thou...knowest not that thou art wretched, and miserable, and poor, and blind, and naked" (v. 17).

E. Exhortation

Jesus first exhorted the Laodicean church to seek true richness — spiritual richness that can be obtained only from Jesus through faith (see v. 18).

Then Jesus said the church should seek from Him a white raiment (see v. 18). This is the robe Jesus clothes us with, signifying our righteousness through His precious shed blood.

Finally, Jesus exhorted the Laodicean church to buy eye salve and anoint its eyes that it might see (see v. 18). This is the eye salve of the Holy Spirit, who opens spiritual eyes. In other words, the church should look at its material and educational wealth through eyes of right self-understanding. Then it would realize that the wealth of the world in which it put so much trust is only transient.

F. Promise

Jesus promised the Laodicean church, "To him that overcometh will I grant to sit with me in my throne, even as I also overcame, and am set down with my Father in his throne" (v. 21). There is no other place to go except the throne of God. This is a wonderful saying, for when we go to the throne of God, the world ends.

G. Interpretation of the Prophecy
   ## (1905 to the beginning of the great tribulation)

In terms of church history, the Laodicean church signifies the age from the 1900s to the time of the great tribulation. *Laodicea* means "the right of laity," namely the church of people's rights. This is a time when the laity have become more "enlightened" than the ministers and when their power is such that they can even hire and fire a pastor at will. Hence, it is a spiritually corrupt age.

From the beginning of the Laodicean age in 1905, theology began to criticize the Bible historically, scientifically and philosophically by introducing rationalism and higher criticism. This started in Germany. The Scripture cannot be subjected to higher criticism through science and reasoning, however, for it was written by divine revelation. Nevertheless, the liberal new theology asserted that the Bible is not scientifically or historically correct; its accounts are mostly myth. Therefore all the miracles in it must be removed.

This new theological thinking began to gain ground in America in the 1920s. It contaminated the pulpits and people, killing many churches just as it had done in Europe. Younger generations left the church, and only the older people remained in them.

Once I heard of a liberal church whose pastor said to the congregation, "Brothers and sisters, the Pentateuch of Moses is the five books of the Bible from Genesis to Deuteronomy; it records the history of Israel in a mythical and instructive way." The members who heard that reasoned, "Why should we carry these heavy books that are merely the mythical history of Israel?" So they removed the Pentateuch from their Bibles.

The next time they attended a service the pastor said, "All the prophetic books in the Bible were written by those who dreamed strange dreams." The members decided, "We now know why they're so complicated," and they cut those parts out of their Bibles.

The next Sunday the pastor said, "The four Gospels of the New Testament are books the disciples of Jesus made up out of extensive delusion to create a new religion with Jesus as its center." So the members removed the Gospels from their Bibles.

When the pastor said, "All the epistles of the New Testament are the personal letters of the apostles that were sent to the churches to revive them," the members removed those parts from their Bibles.

Finally, when the pastor said the Revelation of John was written while the apostle John was in a state of delusion, the members tore *those* pages from their Bibles.

All that remained was the black leather cover that had bound the pages of the Bible together. Then the members left the church, concluding there was nothing believable in God's Word.

Liberal theology leads inevitably to a single conclusion: the death-of-God theory proposed by a theologian named Thomas Altizer. He asserted that since God is dead, humanity should rebuild the church without Him.

Therefore Jesus did not commend the Laodicean church, the church of today, for there was nothing commendable about it. The church has economic strength, many theological schools and much knowledge. However, those don't make it commendable. Rather, liberal churches should buy the eye salve of the Holy Spirit and apply it to their eyes so they can see their spiritual wretchedness, misery, poverty, blindness, nakedness and shame.

God is using the full-gospel movement to help the church regain its faith by opening its eyes. All believers need to return to the pure gospel by purchasing gold tried in fire, putting on the white raiment of righteousness and buying the eye salve that gives spiritual understanding. All the words in the Bible, from Genesis through Revelation, are true, and in them we find God's plan of salvation that brings us to heaven. Those people who keep their faith in this lukewarm age will be taken to the very throne of Christ (see v. 21). Hallelujah!

The word *church* appears seven times in the second and third chapters of Revelation, but it doesn't appear even once in chapters 4-19. Why? Because, as we'll see in chapter 4, Jesus is going to take the church away to that throne in heaven.

TWO

THE RAPTURE OF
THE CHURCH

In Revelation 1:19 John was told to write three things: "the things which thou hast seen, and the things which are, and the things which shall be hereafter." So far we've looked at the first two of those in chapters 1-2 of this book. Now, beginning with Revelation 4, we consider the third, which involves the rapture of the church from earth to heaven into the very presence of the throne of God.

I. A DOOR THAT WAS OPENED
IN HEAVEN (4:1)

> After this I looked, and, behold, a door was
> opened in heaven: and the first voice which I
> heard was as it were of a trumpet talking with
> me; which said, Come up hither, and I will shew
> thee things which must be hereafter (4:1).

The panorama John now viewed had changed from
earth to heaven. Only a short time before, Jesus stood in
the midst of the golden candlesticks and spoke to the
seven churches. That scene disappeared, and when an
awesome gate of heaven was flung open, a voice like a
trumpet said, "Come up hither."

God will likewise use a trumpet sound when He calls
the church to meet Him in the air. We read in 1 Thessalonians 4:16-17:

> For the Lord himself shall descend from heaven
> with a shout, with the voice of the archangel, and
> with the trump of God: and the dead in Christ
> shall rise first: then we which are alive and
> remain shall be caught up together with them in
> the clouds to meet the Lord in the air: and so
> shall we ever be with the Lord.

John was the last surviving apostle. His ascending to
heaven pictures the church at the end of the age that has
prepared oil, being filled with the Holy Spirit (see Matt.
25:1-13), and is taken up into heaven as the bride of
Christ.

It won't be long before that same voice will be heard by
your ears and mine, and we also shall be taken up to
heaven. As a door opened when John looked up, so a door
in heaven will open for us, and we shall also ascend.

Those people who have not been born again by the Holy Spirit, but simply go to church for form and religious ceremony, will not be taken up into heaven. For this reason Jesus said, "Except a man be born of water and of the Spirit, he cannot enter into the kingdom of God" (John 3:5).

The Holy Spirit began the church on earth. When Jesus calls the church in the Spirit to come, the Holy Spirit will take responsibility for that church, taking it to heaven in His bosom.

Nevertheless, many Christians still ask, "Shall we ascend *before* the tribulation, or will we have to pass through it?"

That is a serious question. Some theologians answer that the church will ascend in the *middle* of the tribulation; others say the church will undergo the tribulation. Both those answers are wrong, I believe, ignoring the fact that there are two comings of Christ.

A. Christ's Two Comings

1. Christ's Coming in the Air

The first coming of Christ is His coming in the air as described in 1 Thessalonians 4. This coming is not for the people who belong to the world but for those who have looked forward to this event and prepared for it. The day and the hour of Christ's coming in the air is known to no one (see Luke 12:40). Jesus, our bridegroom, will come and take away His bride. This coming is not one of judgment, but to receive and take His bride away.

Jesus' feet do not touch the earth at this coming; the Bible says clearly that He will receive us in the air (see 1 Thess. 4:17). The dead in Christ will rise all at once and meet Him with resurrected bodies, and we who are living will be changed in a moment. Thus all will ascend into heaven as dew goes up into the sky in the heat of the morning sun.

This coming of Christ in the air will be wonderful. Those who do not participate in it must go through the tribulation, but many of them will also be saved, as we'll see a little later in Revelation.

2. Christ's Coming to Earth

Revelation 19-20 tells us that when the last day of the earth comes near, after the battle of Armageddon, Jesus will come down to earth accompanied by a multitude of His saints. That is His coming to earth. During that time Jesus will destroy all His enemies with a sword that comes out of His mouth. He will take the Antichrist and cast him into the lake of fire, burning with brimstone. He will lay hold of the devil and cast him into the bottomless pit, and He will reign with the saints for a thousand years. This coming of Christ to earth will be visible to everyone, as recorded in Revelation 1:7.

Regrettably, even though the Bible makes a clear distinction between the two comings of Christ, some people are still mistaken in interpreting what will happen. When they teach that the church will also go through the tribulation, they not only hurt themselves but also lead others astray.

B. Biblical Proofs of a Pre-tribulation Rapture of the Church

There are several proofs that the church will not pass through the tribulation. First, because we are in Christ, we cannot be judged a second time. Our sins were judged at the cross of Calvary, borne by the sinless Savior. By offering His own body as a sacrifice, He made all who believe in Him justified and perfect before God.

The tribulation is a seven-year period of the most dreadful nature that will come to those wicked people who rebelled against God and forsook the path of faith. If the church were to pass through it, we would undergo a second judgment, as if Jesus' sacrifice were not sufficient to justify us, and that's impossible. Therefore the Holy Spirit will translate the church before the tribulation.

Second, we see a pattern of what will happen in the stories of Noah and Sodom and Gomorrah. Let's look first at the time of Noah (see Gen. 6-8).

Following Noah's repeated cry that God would judge the world, the flood finally came and lasted forty days and forty nights. Just before that, however, He caused the eight members of Noah's family to enter the ark and escape the flood. *Then* God judged. Jesus said, "But as the days of Noah were, so shall also the coming of the Son of man be" (Matt. 24:37).

God let Noah and his family escape the flood by taking refuge in the ark before He judged the world. How much more will He make a way of escape from the tribulation for those whom Jesus Christ bought with the price of His own blood and sealed with the Holy Spirit? It would be contrary to God's nature for Him to make no distinction between His saints and the rest of the world, judging us the same as He judges them.

Consider also Sodom and Gomorrah. Though Lot lived there by his own free will, yet God, knowing him to be a righteous man, spared the lives of Lot and his family when He rained down judgment. Not until angels had led them safely away did He loose the fire and brimstone (see Gen. 19:15-29).

Thus God rescues those whom He has chosen and who have trusted in Him by faith. And so shall we who have been justified by the precious blood of Jesus escape the tribulation.

Third, the fact that the church is mentioned often in Revelation 1-3, but not once in chapters 4-19, also suggests it will not pass through the tribulation. If we *were* going to endure it, we would surely find references to the church in those chapters. The word *saint* is used often, however, in those chapters. It may refer to people who become Christians after the rapture. At least by its silence, then, this portion of Revelation strongly suggests the church will not pass through the tribulation.

Fourth, Jesus indicated the church will not pass through the tribulation in Luke 21:34-36:

> And take heed to yourselves, lest at any time your hearts be overcharged with surfeiting, and drunkenness, and cares of this life, and so that day come upon you unawares. For as a snare shall it come on all them that dwell on the face of the whole earth. Watch ye therefore, and pray always, that ye may be accounted worthy to escape all these things that shall come to pass, and to stand before the Son of man.

Did Jesus say we should make preparations to pass through all the things that will happen to us? No. He said we must watch and pray so that we may escape all the things that will happen and so stand before Him.

First Thessalonians 1:10 also tells us to "wait for his Son from heaven, whom he raised from the dead, even Jesus, which delivered us from the wrath to come." If He delivered us from the wrath to come, how could He also make us go through it? In Revelation 3:10 Jesus also said to the Philadelphian church, "Because thou hast kept the word of my patience, *I also will keep thee from the hour of temptation,* which shall come upon all the world, to try them that dwell upon the earth" (emphasis added).

When we take into account all these scriptures and

teachings of Jesus, we can conclude with certainty that Jesus will not bring the tribulation of judgment to this world until He completely translates His church at His first coming in the air.

My purpose in writing this book is not to teach you how to pass skillfully through the tribulation, nor is it to teach you with what resolution you should pass through. Rather I want to stimulate you to watch and pray by showing you sure proof that you will be caught up in the air before the tribulation.

II. A THRONE IN HEAVEN (4:2-11)

A. One Who Was Sitting on the Throne

As John looked into heaven, he first saw someone sitting on a throne (see v. 2). The center of heaven is the throne of God, and on it are the Father, the Son and the Spirit. John thus described the figure of God the Father on the throne: "And he that sat was to look upon like a jasper and a sardine stone: and there was a rainbow round about the throne, in sight like unto an emerald" (v. 3).

Jasper signifies the inscrutable divinity and holiness of God. A jasper is a precious, sometimes blue stone — blue like the sky. The sky signifies infinite divinity and holiness.

The ruby-colored sardine stone signifies righteous judgment. When John first saw God, he felt not only the infinite divinity and holiness of God but also His sternness of righteous judgment. John's heart might well have trembled with awesome fear.

The rainbow around the throne resembled an emerald. When we see a rainbow from the earth, it looks like a half-circle. But when we see it from an airplane in the sky, it looks like a complete circle. The sight must have filled John's trembling heart with joy.

The origin of the rainbow goes back to the days of Noah. When Noah sacrificed animals after the flood, God made a covenant with him, saying He would not judge the world again with a flood. As a sign of this covenant, God made a rainbow to appear in the clouds.

Thus, a rainbow resembling an emerald and surrounding the throne means that God, in spite of His infinite divinity and holiness, has already accepted a sacrifice for our sins. That offering is Jesus Christ, the Lamb of God, who died on the cross of Calvary. By accepting Jesus' sacrifice, God made another covenant between Himself and mankind: "Whosoever believeth in him [the only begotten Son of God] should not perish, but have everlasting life" (John 3:16).

B. Twenty-four Elders Around the Throne

After John saw Him who sat on the throne, he also saw twenty-four seats surrounding the throne. Twenty-four elders, with crowns of gold on their heads, sat on those seats. Jesus promised the Laodicean church, "To him that overcometh will I grant to sit with me in my throne, even as I also overcame, and am set down with my Father in his throne" (3:21). Those who overcome will ascend to heaven and sit on the throne that even angels cannot come near.

What do the twenty-four seats signify? I believe they represent the twelve tribes of Israel in the Old Testament and the twelve disciples of Jesus in the New Testament. Altogether the twenty-four seats represent the saints who were saved in both Old and New Testament times.

The twenty-four elders were human beings. Angels cannot have an office such as elder, neither does God give them golden crowns. Such crowns are given only to those who have been saved by the precious blood of Jesus Christ. Imagine in your mind a picture in which you are praising God and wearing a golden crown at His throne. How glorious it will be!

C. The Throne

John also saw "lightnings and thunderings and voices" proceed out of the throne (v. 5). What comes after a flash of lightning and peals of thunder in a summer storm? A shower. God is ready to rain judgment upon this earth like a summer shower. But He is postponing His judgment until His children are taken away to heaven and seated with Him.

Do you know how much God loves you? The love of God toward us is the same sort of love that parents have toward their children, only much stronger. During one overseas trip, a member of my company told me, "Pastor, at this moment I am married and have children, but it seems to me I could not dare sacrifice my life for my parents or wife. However, for the sake of my children I could do it." Because of that kind of love, the holy Son Jesus died on the cross, so now God will not judge the world until He translates all His children to His throne.

"There were seven lamps of fire burning before the throne, which are the seven Spirits of God" (v. 5). This image shows the Holy Spirit on the throne in heaven, having returned there with the church.

In front of the throne was a sea of glass. The sea can be interpreted to mean either mankind or the world. This world, which we call "the troubled sea" because of its many cares and worries, will then be changed into a sea of glass, calm and serene. That means all our tears, cares and troubles will no longer exist.

D. The Four Beasts

Next John saw four beasts around the throne of God and the thrones of the elders (see vv. 6-8). The first was like a lion and the second like a calf; the third had a face like a man, and the fourth was like an eagle. They were praising the Lord God Almighty, saying, "Holy, holy, holy."

Isaiah saw a similar vision. He wrote of seraphim standing above the throne: "Each one had six wings; with twain he covered his face, and with twain he covered his feet, and with twain he did fly. And one cried unto another, and said, Holy, holy, holy, is the Lord of hosts" (Is. 6:2-3).

Ezekiel also saw four living creatures in his vision. Each had four faces that looked like this: "They four had the face of a man, and the face of a lion, on the right side: and they four had the face of an ox on the left side; they four also had the face of an eagle.... And they went every one straight forward" (Ezek. 1:10,12).

What were the four living creatures in Revelation 4? They were cherubim, the angels that guard the holiness of God at His throne. The first was like a lion. That symbolizes Jesus' coming as the King of the Jews, as Matthew's Gospel describes Him. The second creature was like an ox, which signifies Jesus who works, as Mark's Gospel emphasizes. The third creature was like a man, and Luke's Gospel describes Jesus as the Son of man. He had a complete human nature, being born of the virgin Mary. The fourth creature was like an eagle, and the eagle represents the divinity of God. John's Gospel emphasizes that Jesus was the divine Son of God.

Thus, the four living creatures standing around the throne all symbolize the Person of Jesus.

E. Worship

What comes next is a scene of worship. First the four living creatures worship God day and night, never resting. They ceaselessly say, "Holy, holy, holy, Lord God Almighty, which was, and is, and is to come" (v. 8).

And when the living creatures give glory to God, the twenty-four elders also fall down and worship Him. They lay their crowns before the throne and say, "Thou art worthy, O Lord, to receive glory and honour and power: for thou hast created all things, and for thy pleasure they are and were created" (v. 11).

This is the scene of heavenly worship in Revelation 4.

THREE

THE SEVEN-SEALED BOOK

In Revelation 5 the scene changes from heavenly worship to preparation for the great tribulation and judgment.

I. THE SEVEN-SEALED SCROLL (5:1)

And I saw in the right hand of him that sat on the throne a book written within and on the backside, sealed with seven seals. And I saw a strong angel proclaiming with a loud voice, Who is worthy to open the book, and to loose the seals thereof? And no man in heaven, nor in earth, neither under the earth, was able to open the book, neither to look thereon (5:1-3).

John wept bitterly, for there was no one worthy to open the sealed book.

A. A Redemption for the Land

What is this book? Again we must be cautious, for if we wrongly interpret this passage we will miss the whole meaning of the book of Revelation. We can guess the importance of the sealed book from the way its need to be opened was proclaimed and from John's weeping because there was no one worthy to do the job.

This scroll was a title-deed. In Old Testament times God gave this commandment to the Israelites concerning the land they would possess in Canaan:

> The land shall not be sold for ever: for the land is mine; for ye are strangers and sojourners with me. And in all the land of your possession ye shall grant a redemption for the land. If thy brother be waxen poor, and hath sold away some of his possession, and if any of his kin come to redeem it, then shall he redeem that which his brother sold (Lev. 25:23-25).

If a person bought a piece of land from his neighbor, that land became his possession. However, if the closest relative of the original owner came and wanted to repurchase the land, the present owner had to accept that claim no matter how much he desired to keep the land. This law was called "the redemption of the land."

The contract recording a sale of property was a title-deed. After the first article was written, the scroll was rolled and sealed with wax and a stamp. Then the second article was recorded, the same sealing procedure was followed, and so on through every new article. The purpose was to protect the contract from counterfeits. The sealed original was taken to the temple and kept in its archives. A copy of the contract was laid open on a document inspection stand in the temple.

If a kinsman of the original owner read the conditions of such a contract and wanted to buy the land back, he could approach the present owner. If he produced proof that he was a close relative of the original owner and asked to repurchase the land, the present owner had to cooperate. First the kinsman gave the amount of silver and gold specified in the contract to the present owner. Then he went to the temple archives, found the scroll of the contract and opened its seals. Opening one seal, he made sure the conditions of the contract were being met. Then he opened another seal and checked again. During this time he would have several leading people of his village there as witnesses.

After the satisfaction of the contract terms had been thus confirmed before the witnesses and the former and new owners of the land, the change of ownership was declared, and the scroll was burned. With that the transfer of the land was complete.

B. A Scroll With Seven Seals
   in the Hand of God

What kind of title-deed was the scroll in the hand of God? It was the title to ownership of this earth. Before Adam fell into sin, God had given him dominion over, or control of, the earth. When sin came in, however, the earth was corrupted and became the domain of the evil one. Satan was making a valid offer to Jesus in Luke 4:5-7:

> And the devil, taking him up into an high mountain, shewed unto him all the kingdoms of the world in a moment of time. And the devil said unto him, All this power will I give thee, and the glory of them: for that is delivered unto me; and to whomsoever I will I give it. If thou therefore wilt worship me, all shall be thine.

Adam had forfeited his dominion over the world to Satan, in effect making a title-deed of this world before God. And how has the devil used his power? He instigates bloody wars; he foments robbery, abuse and murder. For this reason Paul said, "For we know that the whole creation groaneth and travaileth in pain together until now. And not only they, but ourselves also, which have the firstfruits of the Spirit, even we ourselves groan within ourselves, waiting for the adoption, to wit, the redemption of our body" (Rom. 8:22-23).

Therefore if humanity was to have any hope, someone had to repurchase this earth.

II. No Man Able to Open the Sealed Scroll (5:2-4)

A. Qualifications

The one who could open the scroll had to be a close kinsman to the original "owner" of the world. Thus, the one who would redeem the earth from the devil had to be a human being. But how could sinful people, descendants of Adam, be qualified for this job? In addition, whoever would redeem the earth would have to want to do it enough to pay the price.

Who then would have all these four qualifications: (1) a kinsman to human beings; (2) not a descendant of Adam; (3) able to redeem the earth; and (4) willing to pay the price? The person could not be found in heaven, for the angels are not close kinsmen to us. Nor could the person be found among ordinary, sinful mortals. And the person certainly wouldn't be found under the earth, where devils and evil spirits are, for they would be the last to desire to redeem the earth.

B. The Wailing of John

Thus, there was no one able to open the book and look at it, and John wept bitterly as he realized there was no hope for human beings on the earth. He also wept over his own incompetence in that situation, because he, too, was a member of the fallen human race.

III. THE LION OF THE TRIBE OF JUDAH, THE ROOT OF DAVID (5:5-14)

A. A Lamb That Was Slain

While John was thus weeping, one of the elders said to him, "Weep not: behold, the Lion of the tribe of Judah, the Root of David, hath prevailed to open the book, and to loose the seven seals thereof" (v. 5).

Then John saw that in the midst of the throne, the four beasts and the elders, stood a Lamb. Jesus appeared not as the Son of God but as a Lamb, the sacrifice for sin. The Greek word for this lamb is *arnion*, a lovely little lamb.

On the night before the Israelites left Egypt, they slaughtered Passover lambs and put the blood on the sides and tops of their door frames before eating the meat. Those lambs may have been like family pets, making it painful for everyone when the day came to take a knife and slaughter them.

Jesus Christ was such a lovely little lamb in the sight of God. How pained was the Father's heart when He delivered His Son to be killed, the Son who was the brightness of His glory and the express image of His Person!

Therefore when God commanded the Israelites to kill the Passover lamb, He was foreshadowing the sacrificial death of Christ and the pain He would bear.

Moreover, verse 6 describes Jesus as "a Lamb as it had been slain." Our Lord forever bears the marks of the death He tasted for our sake — the mark of the nails in His hands and feet, of the thorns on His head and of the spear in His side. Whenever we see those marks, we will worship and give thanks to Him for His abounding grace.

B. Seven Horns and Seven Eyes

When John saw this lovely, scarred Lamb come to the throne of almighty God and take the scroll, he noticed the Lamb had seven horns (see v. 6). Since horns symbolize strength, the seven horns represent the authority and strength of a ruler; Jesus has all the power and authority of heaven and earth. The Lamb also had seven all-seeing eyes, which symbolize the Holy Spirit.

C. The Lion of the Tribe of Judah

Also described in verse 5 as the Lion of the tribe of Judah, Jesus met all four conditions for redeeming the earth.

First, to be a close kinsman of human beings — one of us — He left His throne in heaven and became a man, born of the young woman Mary in Bethlehem.

Second, to not be a sin-tainted descendant of Adam, He was supernaturally conceived and born of a virgin. The Bible clearly says in Isaiah 7:14, "Behold, a virgin shall conceive, and bear a son, and shall call his name Immanuel." The angel told Mary, "The Holy Ghost shall come upon thee, and the power of the Highest shall overshadow thee: therefore also that holy thing which shall be born of thee shall be called the Son of God" (Luke 1:35). Therefore Jesus was free from the original sin of Adam and lived a perfect life.

Jesus met the third condition, the ability to redeem the earth by virtue of His sinlessness. It freed Him to take the punishment we deserved for our sins upon Himself (see Rom. 5).

Fourth, Jesus *wanted* to redeem the earth. For all His ability, if Jesus had not wanted to redeem us enough to go to the cross, we would have remained in sin. Yet He voluntarily gave up His life for us. And thus did He rightfully take the title-deed of the earth from the hand of God.

When Jesus received the scroll, His identification as the Lion of the tribe of Judah symbolized His reign as the King of kings. And when our Lord receives the scroll from the Father and tears it open, judgment will have already started. The final work of redeeming the earth will have begun. But the devil will resist with all his might for seven years, knowing the lake of fire awaits him if he loses. At the end of that period of tribulation, however, he will indeed be driven from the earth.

In a sense, Jesus has already taken the scroll, paying for it with His blood. And we don't know the time or season when He will come to claim His purchase; neither do we know when the great tribulation will begin.

One thing is certain, however: When the sound of the trumpet is heard, the saints who have been saved by Jesus' blood will not be on this earth. They will have already been taken up into heaven to attend the marriage supper of the Lamb!

Those who are saved during the tribulation will have suffered great misery. But those who still remain on the earth at the end of the tribulation will be even more miserable. They will weep bitterly when Jesus comes down to this earth with His saints to reign in the millennial kingdom.

D. The Song of the Living Creatures and of the Elders (5:9-10)
(The song of the redeemed saints in heaven)

The saints will sing a song when Jesus takes the scroll with the seven seals from the hand of God:

> You are worthy to take the scroll
>   and to open its seals,
> because you were slain,
>   and with your blood you purchased men for
>   God
>   from every tribe and language and people and
>   nation.
> You have made them to be a kingdom and
>   priests to serve our God,
>   and they will reign on the earth (vv. 9-10,
>   NIV).

Angels are not able to sing such a song. Only the saints can sing this song, because we're the ones Jesus bought with His own blood. And what a wonderful position He's given us as His kingdom and priests — we who have been purchased from every tribe and nation! One day we'll also reign with Him.

E. The Song of the Angels (5:11-12)

Next comes the song of the angels. First notice their position: "And I beheld, and I heard the voice of many angels round about the throne and the beasts and the elders: and the number of them was ten thousand times

70

ten thousand, and thousands of thousands" (v. 11).

The redeemed saints are sitting on the throne; the hosts of angels are standing. As we have learned, the twenty-four elders signify the twelve tribes of Israel and the twelve apostles, which in turn represent all the redeemed saints. As angels were created to serve the redeemed saints (see Heb. 1:14), there is a distinction between the two. They praised Jesus thus: "Worthy is the Lamb that was slain to receive power, and riches, and wisdom, and strength, and honour, and glory, and blessing" (v. 12).

Since the angels have never fallen and were made for a different purpose, their song does not refer to precious blood, being purchased or becoming priests. It's simply a song of praise.

F. The Song of All Creatures (5:13-14)

Following the song of the angels, all creatures sing thus: "Blessing, and honour, and glory, and power, be unto him that sitteth upon the throne, and unto the Lamb for ever and ever" (v. 13).

When all these hymns are ended, the four living creatures respond with "Amen," and the twenty-four elders bow down and worship.

It seems to me that the most beautiful song of the three is the song of the redeemed saints. Isn't God's divine grace wonderful? We're the ones who rebelled against Him and consequently received the greatest love and destiny from God. Part of our response should be beautiful songs of praise to God, and He wants to hear them.

Thus, the preparation for God to reclaim the earth will be completed. As soon as our Lord opens the seals of the scroll, the curtain on the stage of the great tribulation will finally be drawn up.

FOUR

THE GREAT TRIBULATION: PART ONE

O nce again, Revelation 1:19 reads, "Write the things which thou hast seen, and the things which are, and the things which shall be hereafter." We've already considered "the things which thou hast seen" (chapter 1), "the things which are" (chapters 2-3) and the first part of "the things which shall be hereafter" (in chapters 4-5). Now the great tribulation starts in Revelation 6, where our Lord opens the first seal in the book that has seven seals.

How do we know the period of the great tribulation will be seven years? Where in the Bible do we see that time frame given, inasmuch as the exact words *seven years* are not found anywhere in Scripture? The answer is found in the book of Daniel, to which the book of Revelation is closely related. A deeper and clearer understanding can be found by interpreting them together.

I. DANIEL'S SEVENTY WEEKS
(DAN. 9:24-27)

Daniel was one of the Jews taken captive to Babylon when the kingdom of Judah fell in 605 B.C. While reading the book of Jeremiah there, he came across the prophecy that said Israel would return home after seventy years. To know exactly when that would happen, he prayed earnestly to God. An angel of the Lord appeared to him and showed him in detail not only the return of Israel to its land, but also what would happen from then to the end of the world. The following is what the angel told Daniel:

> Seventy weeks are determined upon thy people and upon thy holy city, to finish the transgression, and to make an end of sins, and to make reconciliation for iniquity, and to bring in everlasting righteousness, and to seal up the vision and prophecy, and to anoint the most Holy. Know therefore and understand, that from the going forth of the commandment to restore and to build Jerusalem unto the Messiah the Prince shall be seven weeks, and threescore and two weeks: the street shall be built again, and the wall, even in troublous times. And after threescore and two weeks shall Messiah be cut off, but not for himself: and the people of the prince that shall come shall destroy the city and the sanctuary; and the end thereof shall be with a flood, and unto the end of the war desolations are

determined. And he shall confirm the covenant with many for one week: and in the midst of the week he shall cause the sacrifice and the oblation to cease, and for the overspreading of abominations he shall make it desolate, even until the consummation, and that determined shall be poured upon the desolate (Dan. 9:24-27).

The angel Gabriel came and told Daniel that seventy weeks would be determined upon "thy people," the people of Judah, and "thy holy city," Jerusalem. Since one week in the Bible signifies seven years, seventy weeks is 490 years.

Therefore the prophecy meant that after 490 years had passed, the transgression would be finished, sins would end, reconciliation for iniquity would be made forever, everlasting righteousness would be brought in, all the visions and prophecies would come to pass, and the most Holy — the Messiah, our Lord Jesus Christ — would come to this world to redeem the world.

The angel even predicted the exact time of Jesus' entering Jerusalem, riding on a donkey from the Mount of Olives. The Messiah in verse 25 refers to Jesus Christ. Gabriel said that from the going forth of the commandment to restore and rebuild Jerusalem until the Messiah, the Prince, would be seven weeks and sixty-two weeks, or a total of sixty-nine weeks. And on March 14, 445 years before Jesus was born, King Artaxerxes of Persia gave an order to restore Jerusalem.

As a result, some of the Israelites who had been carried away to Babylon as captives returned home. On April 6, A.D. 32, sixty-nine weeks or 483 years after that, Jesus entered Jerusalem on a donkey, so the prophecy was fulfilled precisely. (This includes leap years.)

Out of the seventy weeks in Daniel 9:24, sixty-nine have already passed. In verse 27 we have the record of just one week. Again, one week signifies seven years. "He" mentioned in verse 27 refers to a Roman emperor who will appear at the end of the world (the Antichrist). He will confirm the covenant with many Jews for seven years. However, in the middle of that period, after three and one-half years, he will break the covenant and cause the worship of the Jews to cease. Thus, during the first part of the great tribulation the persecution will be less intense.

During the second three and one-half years, the Antichrist will completely break the covenant with the Jews. He will enter the temple and claim to be the king. This will be the period of severe tribulation, but "that determined" (God's wrath) will be poured upon "the desolate" (the Antichrist).

In Daniel 9:26 is a prophecy about what would happen during the church age after the resurrection of Jesus. A Roman general named Titus came with his army and destroyed Jerusalem in A.D. 70, fulfilling the part of the prophecy saying "the people of the prince that shall come shall destroy the city and the sanctuary." At the end of the church age, which has so far lasted two thousand years, the Antichrist will appear and begin the great tribulation.

Daniel 9 has deeper theological implications that go beyond the scope of this book, but I trust you can see now why scholars conclude the great tribulation will be seven years long. It will be the last period in which God exhorts the Jews, His chosen people, to repent. For the gentiles it will be a period in which they betray Jesus Christ and go through torment and destruction to the end. Let's look now at what will happen during the great tribulation.

II. OPENING OF THE SEALS (6:1-17)

A. The First Seal and the Man Who Rode on the White Horse (6:1-2)

As John in the Spirit watched these future events unfold, Jesus opened the first of the seven seals on the scroll. Then one of the four living creatures, with a voice like thunder, said to John, "Come and see."

John looked and saw "a white horse: and he that sat on him had a bow; and a crown was given unto him: and he went forth conquering, and to conquer" (v. 2).

1. The Man Who Rode on the White Horse Was Not Jesus

It's easy to make the mistake of interpreting this figure riding on a white horse to be Jesus. The great tribulation had already begun, however, and Jesus was in heaven, opening the first seal. Therefore to suppose that Jesus rode on a white horse and "went forth conquering, and to conquer" doesn't fit the time sequence, nor is it acceptable from a logical point of view. There are several reasons this must take place at the outset of the tribulation.

First, the church has already been carried into heaven. Jesus works through the church and the Holy Spirit, but as we saw in Revelation 4, the church has already gone through the open door of heaven, accompanied by the Holy Spirit. Hence, the age of grace, the church age, has ended. Therefore, to interpret 6:2 as saying Jesus appears again, riding on a white horse and preaching the gospel ("conquering, and to conquer"), at the beginning of the tribulation is not reasonable chronologically.

Second, the man on a white horse goes forth conquering with a bow, but Jesus is clearly identified in Revelation 19 as fighting with a sword that comes out of His mouth (see 19:15). As that passage shows, such a weapon is enough.

Third, Revelation 19:12 says that on the head of Jesus, the King of kings, were many crowns. The man who rides on a white horse wears only one crown.

Fourth, Jesus has already won the victory and will come next to the earth to judge. He has no need to fight belatedly, "conquering, and to conquer." He wrote to the church in Laodicea, "To him that overcometh will I grant to sit with me in my throne, even as I also overcame, and am set down with my Father in his throne" (3:21).

Therefore he who rode on a white horse is not Jesus.

2. He Who Rode on a White Horse Is the Antichrist

Who then is riding on a white horse? None other than the Antichrist, disguising himself as Jesus Christ, falsely claiming he is the messiah who will bring peace and prosperity to the world. The title "antichrist" is put on him because he pretends to be Christ. For that purpose he rides a white horse (which symbolizes purity and victory), wears a crown and has a bow in his hand to conquer. Figuratively speaking, this is the same as a spy who, having infiltrated enemy territory, pretends to be a citizen of the foreign land by imitating the language and customs of the people and by wearing their clothes.

Thus, the Antichrist will come as a self-styled messiah, and the whole world will exalt and welcome him.

I believe this Antichrist has already been born. Perhaps he was born someplace in Europe or in the Middle East and is now attending a university, or perhaps he has already started his career as a politician. And if he is indeed already in this world, the day of our going to heaven is nearer than we may think.

One thing we should notice in Rev. 6:2 is that there is

no mention of arrows with his bow. The Antichrist will take possession of the white horse of victory and the crown of glory — the position of a top leader — not by the means of war, but by his subtle political and diplomatic ability.

By using some trick, he will put all the countries in a united Europe under his control. At first he will have only three countries in his hand by taking them out by their roots; then the rest of the seven countries will surrender to him. In this way he will unify the ten European countries in the former territory of Rome.

When Europe comes under the banner of one union, it will possess enormous power economically as well as militarily, and the whole world will kneel down to it. When the Antichrist appears, however, he will make a covenant with Israel for seven years, as we saw in Daniel 9:24-27. Accordingly, the day when the united nations of Europe and Israel ratify a seven-year contract is the very day when the first seal of the tribulation is opened.

If people read in the morning newspaper one day that the president of the united nations of Europe has concluded a seven-year treaty of friendship and prosperity with Israel, they will be sorry, because they were not caught up into heaven. I pray in the name of our Lord that you will not be among them.

Is the world situation really going in the direction of producing the seven-year treaty between Europe and Israel? First let's consider Israel's perspective. The Jews, who had wandered for two thousand years, miraculously regained their state of Israel on May 14, 1948. That was a miracle of miracles indeed.

Can you imagine the difficulty a nation would face in regaining its lost territory after two thousand years? Try to feel that through your imagination. In Korean history, Ko-gu-ryu, an old kingdom of our ancestors located in the northern part of the Korean Peninsula, once possessed the territory reaching to Manchuria. With the fall of the kingdom in 668, however, Ko-gu-ryu lost her vast domain to the kingdoms of Silla and Tiang. Since then, Korea has never regained that territory in Manchuria. If we should now ask Communist China to return that territory thirteen hundred years later, do you think she would accede to our request? Would such a thing ever be possible?

Nevertheless, Israel regained her land after two thousand years. If that's not a miracle of God, what is? He granted it in order to accomplish His preordained will, gathering dispersed Jews from all over the world.

God has also preserved Israel through several wars in which Arab states, with a collective population of over 200 million, struggled to swallow the tiny nation of Israel, which has a mere three million people. These, too, were miracles. Though the enormous group of Arab nations, like a lion, has tried to devour Israel, which is like a mouse by comparison, every time the lion has been beaten by the mouse.

Europeans began to be concerned when World War II ended and they found themselves sandwiched between the mighty military and economic strength of the United States and the U.S.S.R. To enhance their position, their leaders concluded that all the nations in Europe (the former territory of Rome) should work together at various levels.

In 1958, ten years after Israel became an independent nation, the European Economic Community was formed, with its capital in Brussels, Belgium. Since that time, progress in economic cooperation has given rise to plans for military and political unity as well. Europe becomes a union economically in 1992.

When this unification is complete, the people of the countries belonging to the EEC will not need passports when traveling to other countries within the bloc. They will cross the borders freely and hold the jobs they want in other countries.

Thus, Europe has largely achieved economic unification through the EEC, and a high degree of military coordination has come about through the North Atlantic Treaty Organization. Now, if they achieve political unification, the so-called United Nations of Europe will be complete.

The establishment of a Jewish state has been accomplished. The unification of Europe is progressing steadily. Since everything thus proceeds according to the prophecy of the Bible, we can conclude that the coming of our Lord is at hand.

When Europe is unified politically and the Antichrist takes over, he will make the treaty with Israel for whatever reason — perhaps with the intention of betraying the Jews from the start. Why would Israel make such a treaty? Maybe its leaders will think a strong Europe can help it rebuild the temple in Jerusalem. Many Jews are eager to resurrect Solomon's temple, which was destroyed and replaced by a Muslim mosque (the Dome of the Rock). Those Jews want to pull down the mosque and build their own temple there. If they try to do that, however, the two billion Muslims all over the world will rise to protest, and war will inevitably break out. The power and influence of the Antichrist may be so great, however, that the Jews will think he can help them fulfill their dream.

Whatever their exact reasoning at the time, both parties will find usefulness in each other and so agree to help one another. And their treaty will mark the beginning of the end.

B. The Second Seal and the Red Horse (6:3-4)

When the Lamb of God opened the second seal, John

saw a red horse coming, "and power was given to him that sat thereon to take peace from the earth, and that they should kill one another: and there was given unto him a great sword" (v. 4). That red horse symbolizes war and blood. A horrible carnage now takes place.

In the day Israel tries to pull down the Dome of the Rock in Jerusalem and rebuild Solomon's temple in its place, the entire Arab world will launch an all-out offensive against Israel. That mosque is the second most sacred place of the Muslims, so how could they stand by idly while an attempt was being made to demolish it? Following their lead, Russia will also attack Israel.

This has been foretold in Ezekiel 38. According to that prophecy, Russia will invade like the surge of a sea and fight against Israel, but it will be defeated miserably in the end. Then Israel will freely build its temple. Hence, the bloody war that will break out with the opening of the second seal is a war between Israel and the Arabs and Russia. A great number of people will be killed. It is also prophesied that Israel will rise to be a powerful country and will cooperate with the unified Europe for three and one-half years.

I believe the red horse also signifies communism, which is symbolized by the color red.

C. The Third Seal and the Black Horse (6:5-6)

When the third seal was opened, John saw a black horse, and its rider had a balance in his hands. This is a time of great famine. The shortage of food is so severe that its sale will be rationed by being weighed in the balance, "a measure of wheat for a penny, and three measures of barley for a penny; and see thou hurt not the oil and the wine" (v. 6).

Famine and economic ruin are always the aftermath of

war. During the war, resources are consumed by the war effort, as are available workers, and industrial facilities are destroyed.

The rider of the black horse is forbidden, however, to harm cooking oil and wine. Why? I believe it's because olive oil and wine are precious things used for sacrifices to God. But apart from them there will be a dreadful famine and economic devastation.

Even today, when there is no major war, many parts of the world face a severe food shortage. Experts say a worldwide famine would cost fifty million lives a year. I sincerely pray that all of you who read this book will be in heaven when the famine foretold in verse 6 occurs.

D. The Fourth Seal and the Pale Horse (6:7-8)

The mention of the horse's color makes us shudder. Its rider's name is Death. *Hades*, or hell, means in this case a public cemetery. The war will take many lives, and the famine and epidemics that follow will take even more.

Our Lord said in Matthew 24:7-8, "For nation shall rise against nation, and kingdom against kingdom: and there shall be famines, and pestilences, and earthquakes, in divers places. All these are the beginning of sorrows." We read in Revelation 6:8b, "And power was given unto them [Death and Hell] over the fourth part of the earth, to kill with sword, and with hunger, and with death, and with the beasts of the earth."

Since the population of the world is now five billion, one-fourth of that is 1.25 billion people. During the first three and one-half years of the great tribulation, more than one billion people will die on account of war and its aftermath and be buried in public cemeteries. The present population of China is one billion. Can you imagine what a huge number that is? Therefore the pale horse signifies terrible disasters.

E. The Fifth Seal and the Martyrs (6:9-11)

The "souls of them that were slain for the word of God, and for the testimony which they held" (v. 9) are the people who become martyrs during the first three and one-half years of the great tribulation. They are said to be "under the altar." Since the altar is the place where sacrifices are offered, they are there as a sacrifice offered to God. They weep bitterly and plead to God that He will take His revenge quickly. If they had earlier believed in Jesus Christ and been caught up into heaven, how much better it would have been for them!

But then Jesus gives them white robes. Those are given to comfort them. And Jesus tells them they should rest yet for a while until their "fellow servants" and "their brethren, that should be killed as they were, should be fulfilled" (v. 11).

Here we find that God continues His work of salvation even while the tribulation is going on, like a farmer gleaning ears of grain, because if one more soul can be saved, God wills to do it.

F. The Sixth Seal and the Disasters in Nature (6:12-17)

As soon as the sixth seal is opened, fearful things will happen on the earth and in heaven. A great earthquake will take place, the sky will become pitch black with volcanic ash, and the moon will become red due to the ash and dust (see v. 12). The sky will be rolled together like a scroll (see v. 14). So severe will the earthquake be that every mountain and island will be moved out of its place, and the stars will fall out of the sky (see v. 13).

When such phenomena occur, everyone from kings to slaves will hide themselves in caves and in the rocks of the mountains. They will cry to those mountains and rocks: "Fall on us, and hide us from the face of him that sitteth on the throne, and from the wrath of the Lamb: for the great day of his wrath is come; and who shall be able to stand?" (vv. 16-17).

Notice that in spite of such terrible happenings, those people still do not repent to God but pray to the rocks and stones. People are so foolish! God wants to deliver them, but they won't repent. What a heartbreaking scene that will be!

Six seals have been opened thus far. Between the sixth seal and the seventh, a parenthetical scene appears, and we see God sealing those preachers who will deliver the remaining people on earth during the first half of the great tribulation.

III. PARENTHETIC: SEALING OF GOD'S SERVANTS (7:1-17)

A. The Angels Holding the Winds of the Earth (7:1)

In Revelation 7:1 John saw "four angels standing on the four corners of the earth, holding the four winds of the earth, that the wind should not blow on the earth, nor on the sea, nor on any tree." The wind signifies war, and God commanded the angels in charge of the war to suspend it until all the preachers of the gospel be sealed on their foreheads (see vv. 2-3).

The sealing mentioned here is not the same as the sealing of the Holy Spirit. Our being drawn today to faith in Jesus and to salvation is done by the invisible sealing of the Holy Spirit upon our souls. In that day, however, God's sealing on the foreheads of His servants will be visible to everyone. Later the devils will also seal those who follow the Antichrist with the number 666 on their foreheads or hands.

B. The Preachers of the Gospel Sealed During the Tribulation (7:2-8)

Thus, the sealing of God's servants begins as an angel ascends from the rising of the sun and begins to seal. Some people misinterpret this scene and cause confusion. In Korea, for example, some think it means God will start His sealing with the Korean people, since Korea is located in the East, or toward the rising of the sun. But I do not want to be sealed at that time, because before that happens the Christians will already be in heaven watching events on the earth!

The sun symbolizes Jesus Christ. Accordingly, the verse says the angel comes from the throne of Jesus in obedience to His order.

1. Those Who Are Sealed Are All Jews

Those sealed are the preachers of the gospel who will deliver the remnants of God during the first half of the tribulation. Furthermore, verses 4-8 tell us they're all Jews — 144,000 out of every tribe of the sons of Israel.

Why was the tribe of Dan omitted and the tribe of Manasseh included instead? There's a definite reason for that.

First Kings 12:25-30 describes how idolatry was committed in the northern kingdom of Israel. Jeroboam, its first king, made two golden calves and set one in Dan and the other in Bethel, the hill country of Ephraim. Both the tribes of Dan and Ephraim worshipped the calves. God had said earlier that He would blot out the names of those who serve other gods from under heaven (see Deut.

29:18-20). Therefore the name of Dan was omitted from the list of the twelve tribes of Israel and replaced by the tribe of Manasseh, who was the firstborn of Joseph.

2. *The Wrong Interpretation About the Number 144,000*

Today there are many heretics who deceive people using the number 144,000. Jehovah's Witnesses maintain that only 144,000 people will go to heaven. If that were true, however, that number would already be there, leaving the rest of us without hope. Park Tae-sun, founder of a Korean cult, also asserts that when the number of the saved reaches 144,000, the end of the world will come. That also is a misinterpretation.

3. *144,000: The Servants Who Will Glean the Remaining Souls*

The 144,000 are the Jewish servants of God who will glean the remaining souls in the first half of the tribulation. Why does God choose them for that purpose?

Those who preached the gospel first were Jews. Those who recorded the Bible were also Jews. And it's only right that our Lord would again use His chosen people as those who would complete His kingdom.

These 144,000 Jews are like the seven thousand people God preserved during the time of Elijah; they did not bow their knees to Baal but kept their faith in God to the very end. The end-time Jews will have accepted Jesus Christ as their Savior and entered into salvation. God will seal them for His use as preachers of the gospel, and they will preach it everywhere during the first half of the tribulation.

C. A Great Multitude of People
   Who Will Be Saved (7:9-14)

The 144,000 Jewish preachers will present the gospel so diligently, even sacrificing their lives, that the people who are saved out of all nations and peoples can't be numbered. As John saw them, they "stood before the throne, and before the Lamb, clothed with white robes, and palms in their hands" (v. 9).

One of the elders told John, "These are they which came out of great tribulation, and have washed their robes, and made them white in the blood of the Lamb" (v. 14).

Their white robes are proof that they are washed clean by the precious blood of Jesus Christ, and the palm branches they hold are tokens that they overcame the Antichrist and the tribulation. However, the martyrs, as we saw in Revelation 6, were lying flat under the altar. Therefore this great multitude of people standing around the throne did not pass through martyrdom.

The important point for us is that those who rely on the precious blood of Jesus will be saved even in the midst of the tribulation. We must witness diligently for Christ. Even if people don't believe now, they may believe and go to heaven when they are exhorted by the 144,000 preachers.

The time is at hand, so let's be faithful to sow the seed of the gospel. Don't be discouraged if people fail to believe now. Just sow the seed. Jesus will cause it to grow, and many will be saved even after He comes for His church.

D. What Is Implied by the Great
   Multitude Who Are Saved (7:15-17)

The people who go to heaven belatedly do not sit on the throne. They stand before it and give praise to God, waving the palm branches in their hands. They do not wear crowns, nor do they receive rewards, because they did not believe early according to faith. The saints who were already saved, however, receive golden crowns as their rewards.

When God dwells among the saints of the tribulation (see v. 15), they shall hunger no more, neither thirst anymore; neither shall the sun light on them, nor any heat (v. 16).

Because those people went through so much hunger and thirst, God will not make them suffer any longer. The Bible also says they will not hurt any longer. From this we can imagine how much pain they suffer from the Antichrist: "For the Lamb which is in the midst of the throne shall feed them, and shall lead them unto living fountains of waters: and God shall wipe away all tears from their eyes" (v. 17).

IV. THE SEVENTH SEAL AND THE TRUMPETS OF SEVEN ANGELS (8:1-9:21)

There are many symbols in the book of Revelation. That's because John could not explain what he saw through his experience or words, for he saw things that would happen two thousand years in the future. For example, let us suppose a Korean who lived a century ago were to be resurrected and made to stand at Chongro Square in Seoul. He would not know what to call an automobile. How difficult it would be to explain an automobile if you had never seen one before! You might try to describe it as an iron horse rolling along with four legs, with eyes like flashing lamps.

For this reason, in order to understand Revelation, we must make a thorough study of the meaning of John's symbols. Please bear in mind that most of the words we'll study from now on are recorded in symbolic terms.

A. The Seventh Seal (8:1-2)

In the eighth chapter of Revelation is the opening of the seventh seal, followed immediately by seven trumpets. When the seventh trumpet sounds, seven bowls are introduced. It is like a firework that goes off with a loud bang and breaks into seven smaller fireworks; when the seventh of the smaller fireworks goes off, it explodes into still smaller sparks. The first firework can be compared to the seventh seal; the seven smaller fireworks emanating from it are the seven trumpets; and the sparks emanating from the seventh small firework are the seven bowls.

There is important meaning in the statement "There was silence in heaven about the space of half an hour" (v. 1). Even while God executes judgment, He still wants human beings to repent and be gleaned into the salvation of eternal life, freed from the snare of the devil. That is why God waits silently for half an hour. It's a chance for people to throw themselves on His mercy and avoid the approaching judgment that will begin with the opening of the seventh seal.

Moreover, this silence of half an hour is meant to forewarn of a greater coming judgment. You may have felt the same when you scolded your children. When their disobedience is trivial, you quickly scold with a few words. But when the offense is grave, you may just look at them, dumbfounded. When Daddy or Mommy looks into a child's eyes, not saying a word, that is the most awesome and dreadful time for the child, because it means a greater punishment will surely follow. In the same way, the silence of half an hour forewarns of a greater judgment.

B. An Angel Having a Golden Censer (8:3-5)

After the silence of half an hour, the seven angels stand, with each one holding a trumpet. One angel comes with a golden censer full of incense and offers the incense on the altar of God.

This is the holy of holies. In Old Testament times Solomon's temple contained the holy place and, behind a curtain, the holy of holies. Entrance to the holy place was restricted to the high priest alone, and even he could enter the holy of holies only once a year, and that not without blood. The holy of holies is where God dwells.

John saw there an angel who was about to offer incense. Who is this angel?

Since angels do not have the priesthood, none of them can become the high priest. The priesthood was reserved for Aaron and his descendants. There is another person, however, who has become a priest in the order of Melchizedek. He is Jesus Christ, our high priest (see Heb. 7:20-22). Therefore I believe it is Jesus who offers the incense from the golden censer on the altar of God.

The incense Jesus received was offered with the prayers of the saints (see vv. 3-4). As our high priest, Jesus still carries out the work of receiving prayers of the saints and offering them on the altar of God. As the high priest who offers sacrifice for us, He also never stops praying for us.

You may be trying to settle in your own mind what is meant by the prayers of the saints, if the saints are already in heaven. One thing you must know for sure is that saints pray not only when they're on the earth, but also when they're in heaven. The Bible clearly calls us "a royal priesthood" (1 Pet. 2:9). And since part of the job of priests is to intercede for others, we'll pray all the more while we're in heaven. Therefore the saints in heaven are praying for the salvation of more souls on the earth, and the remaining souls on earth pray that they may be gleaned into salvation. To those prayers is added the intercessory prayer of Jesus, and thus the golden censer becomes full of the incense of prayers.

Throughout my ministry I have seen a wonderful thing occur. Namely, when Christian parents die leaving non-Christian children behind, the non-Christian children usually accept the faith soon afterward. Even the most stubborn children who used to oppose the evangelism of their parents will usually come to believe in Jesus.

Why does this happen? I believe it's because Christian parents continue to pray fervently in heaven for the souls of their children on earth. Even at this moment the saints who went to heaven before us are praying to Jesus for you and me, asking that the will of the Lord be done on this earth. The prayers turn into incense that is put into the golden censer, and it ascends before the throne of God. Hearing those prayers, God responds by drawing unsaved loved ones to Himself.

The next scene shows that the angel took the censer, filled it with fire from the altar and hurled it onto the earth, followed by peals of thunder, rumblings, flashes of lightning and an earthquake. That means Jesus receives our prayers, offers them to God and, as the high priest who prays for us, receives an answer from the Father and brings it to the world.

From this point God will avenge the martyred saints. Therefore we must not stop praying, for our prayers surely turn into incense as they ascend before His throne; and His answers come down and are fulfilled in our lives.

C. The Trumpet of the First Angel (8:7)

When the seventh seal is opened, the first angel sounds

the trumpet. This scene will unfold in the first half of the tribulation. With the sound of the trumpet, "there followed hail and fire mingled with blood, and they were cast upon the earth: and the third part of trees was burnt up, and all green grass was burnt up."

What does that mean? As I said before, John had to write this way because, in his age, there were no modern weapons — arms such as the bow and spear were all he knew.

However, we can now speculate that in all probability John was describing the effects of a hydrogen bomb. Today such a weapon can devastate a wide area, burning all the trees and grass in its way. When an atomic bomb was dropped on Hiroshima, Japan, in August 1945, there was a sudden downpour of hail. That happened because the air heated by the explosion went up with the vapor, and as it was cooled in the high altitude of the atmosphere, it turned into hail and fell to the earth. To John, the explosion of numerous nuclear bombs might well have looked like "hail and fire mingled with blood."

I conclude, therefore, that this scripture shows that a devastating nuclear war will occur during the first half of the tribulation. God will judge this world through human hands. At present, the United States, Russia, France, China, India and others are all manufacturing and stockpiling nuclear weapons. The day will come when they'll use them. We must remember that since human history began, mankind has never made a weapon it did not use. Enough nuclear bombs have already been made to destroy the earth several times. One-quarter of the world's population will die during that time, possibly due to nuclear weapons.

The burning of one-third of the earth's vegetation will also cause food shortages. Moreover, the destruction of the third part of the trees will greatly damage air quality, since trees purify air by turning carbon dioxide into oxygen.

Air pollution is already a major problem in the world today. How much more of a problem will it be then? Such miserable schemes will happen with the sounding of the first trumpet.

D. The Trumpet of the Second Angel (8:8-9)

When the second angel sounds the trumpet, something like a "great mountain" all ablaze is thrown into the sea.

The fulfillment of that prophecy may relate to something the United States and Russia are developing, called the space bus. This device, loaded with atomic and hydrogen warheads, is put into an earth orbit. When a button is pressed on earth, the bus explodes and falls to the ground like a burning volcano. It splits into several hundred or thousand pieces. Accordingly, it can turn a big country into a sea of flames. Some say Russia has already put such a space bus into earth orbit.

When the second angel sounds the trumpet, a third of the living creatures in the sea die, and a third of the ships are destroyed. From this scripture we can imagine the following situation.

A space bus is fired toward the place where enemy warships have gathered, and that whole part of the sea turns into havoc. Not only do warships and merchant ships sink, but a third of the sea's living creatures are killed. That would greatly reduce the earth's transportation capacity and supply of seafood.

E. The Trumpet of the Third Angel (8:10-11)

When the third angel sounded the trumpet, "there fell

a great star from heaven, burning as it were a lamp, and it fell upon the third part of the rivers, and upon the fountains of waters;...and the third part of the waters became wormwood; and many men died of the waters." John thought it was a great star, but my guess is that it was a biological bomb, because the water was polluted, and everyone who drank the water died. This also will happen in the first half of the tribulation, when the Arab nations, backed by Russia, war against Israel and the league of European nations.

F. The Trumpet of the Fourth Angel (8:12)

When the fourth angel sounded the trumpet, a third of the sun, moon and stars turned dark. A third of the day and the night were without light. How could this happen?

If a nuclear war breaks out, burning up a third of all the trees in the world and destroying one-third of all ships, the dust arising from the explosions would sweep over the earth, and the earth would become darkened as if an eclipse of the sun or moon were taking place. Scientifically, this is natural. When a volcano bursts into eruption, the sky gets dark even in the daytime. How much more would it be possible in a nuclear war at the end of the world! Thus, the focus of chapter 8 is on the destruction of the natural environment by the first four angels.

G. The Warning of an Angel (8:13)

Before the fifth angel sounded the trumpet, another angel flew in the midst of the sky, crying, "Woe, woe, woe." It was a warning about the trumpets of the three remaining angels — that is, three dreadful judgments.

H. The Trumpet of the
Fifth Angel (9:1-11)

When the fifth angel sounded the trumpet, John saw a star fall onto the earth. That star was Lucifer, or Satan. Isaiah 14:12 says, "How art thou fallen from heaven, O Lucifer, son of the morning! how art thou cut down to the ground, which didst weaken the nations!"

Satan was given the key of the bottomless pit, where evil spirits are imprisoned. When Jesus cast out demons, they begged Him not to command them to depart into the bottomless pit (see Luke 8:31). However, God put those there who attempted to lift themselves up to the throne of God, not keeping their own positions. The Bible says:

> God spared not the angels that sinned, but cast them down to hell, and delivered them into chains of darkness, to be reserved unto judgment (2 Pet. 2:4).

> And the angels which kept not their first estate, but left their own habitation, he hath reserved in everlasting chains under darkness unto the judgment of the great day (Jude 6).

Since human beings will not repent during the first half of the tribulation, our Lord gives the devil the key to afflict them. When he opens the door to the bottomless pit, there arises a smoke like that from a huge furnace, and the sun is darkened. That may refer to a volcanic eruption.

Out of that dust come hordes of evil spirits that have been shut up there. They had been bound for such a long time that they will be eager to ravage human beings. Among the loosed may be the unclean spirit that afflicted the woman with the issue of blood for twelve years; also perhaps the demon who had made the man roam naked among the tombs. What great havoc they will wreak on the earth!

The Bible describes the spirits as locusts, and "unto them was given power, as the scorpions of the earth have power" (v. 3). Scorpions are creatures with an incredibly sharp sting. They're said to have caused Roman soldiers, famous for their bravery, to cry painfully for help. Roman soldiers were so thoroughly trained that when they were beaten by their superiors, they did not break down, even when their bones were broken. How painful it will be to human beings when demons from the bottomless pit hurt them with the power of scorpions!

However, our Lord commanded that they should not hurt any green thing or the 144,000 Jewish evangelists who have been sealed on their foreheads. The demons cannot touch those whom God has sealed. This is also true today. When we are sealed and armed by the precious blood of Jesus and by the Holy Spirit, demons can't hurt us.

During the five months when the evil spirits afflicted those who were not sealed, their pain was so severe that they wanted to die (see v. 6). However, even though they sought death, God took it away from them so they would have an opportunity to repent. That is the grace of God, for anyone who dies apart from Christ will be cast into the fire of hell.

God had already saved the martyrs who died during the first three and one-half years and were under the altar. After them He saved innumerable people through the testimony of the 144,000 preachers. He will still continue His saving work beyond that, though the faith of those saved may be tiny like a mustard seed, until there remain only those who absolutely will not believe in Christ. This is the infinite love of God.

The appearance of the evil spirits symbolized as locusts

is so ghastly that it surpasses our imagination. "Their faces were as the faces of men. And they had hair as the hair of women, and their teeth were as the teeth of lions. And they had breastplates, as it were breastplates of iron; and the sound of their wings was as the sound of chariots of many horses running to battle. And they had tails like unto scorpions, and there were stings in their tails" (vv. 7-10). Their king was named Apollyon in the Greek language, which means "destroyer." They went everywhere destroying and robbing, but the authority to kill was not given to them. In Revelation 8 John described natural calamities, but in this chapter the judgment on human beings has begun.

I. The Trumpet of the Sixth Angel (9:12-21)

When the sixth angel sounded the trumpet, John heard a voice saying, "Loose the four angels which are bound in the great river Euphrates" (v. 14), which divided the east from the west. This river basin has been a land of rebellion from the beginning of time.

The Euphrates is a branch of the river originating in the Garden of Eden, where Adam sinned (see Gen. 2:14). The first rebellion against God took place there, and it was also the place where Cain, the first murderer, killed his brother, Abel. Moreover, the tower of Babel, that prominent symbol of human rebellion against God, was also built in a place near this river. Idolatrous Babylon was situated along this river. Thus, the valley of the Euphrates has been a place of wicked rebellion against God since the beginning of the world.

God bound four rebellious angels there at some point. When they are loosed during the first half of the tribulation, they are to kill one-third of the world population (see v. 15). When the fourth seal is opened, one-fourth of the world population, or more than one billion people, will die. When one-third of that remaining population is killed, another one billion will die.

Therefore, during the short period of three and one-half years, more than half the population of the world dies, leaving only about two billion people. Imagine how severe the tribulation will be! Blessed are the saints who are caught up into heaven before such a tribulation starts. Hallelujah!

Those four angels cannot kill at any time they choose, however. The hour, the day, the month and the year have already been fixed (see v. 15). Verse 16 says the number of the horsemen is "two hundred thousand thousand," or 200 million. Therefore the four angels will mobilize an army of that size who will cross over the Euphrates.

This is the beginning of the battle of Armageddon that will take place during the second half of the tribulation. It will be explained fully in chapter 6, section 8 of this book.

The only country in the world that can mobilize so great an army is China. In 1961 China announced its military strength as being 200 million (regular forces and militia combined). When John received this revelation, however, the total population of the world was less than that. How amazed John must have been when he heard the number!

In this passage is a picture of modern warfare. In John's day, armies used horses or chariots drawn by horses. Now John saw strange horses and riders with "breastplates of fire, and of jacinth, and brimstone: and the heads of the horses were as the heads of lions; and out of their mouths issued fire and smoke and brimstone" (v. 17). That sounds today like tanks firing their guns, flame-throwers hurling flames, and atomic and hydrogen bombs being dropped from the air. By these weapons a third of the earth's people are killed. Nevertheless, people do not repent of their sins (see vv. 20-21). Why does the Bible mention this? It is to show that God is still waiting for their repentance and conversion. If God thought them hopeless, there would be no need to mention it.

V. PARENTHETICAL (10:1-11)

After such a dreadful second woe following the trumpet of the sixth angel, Revelation 10 reveals parenthetical things that will happen before the judgment of the seven bowls begins with the trumpet of the seventh angel.

A. The Angel Who Sets One Foot on the Sea and One Foot on the Earth (10:1-6)

Verses 1-6 say that a mighty angel set his right foot on the sea and his left foot on the earth. Who was this angel? Notice how he is described. He came down from heaven, clothed with a cloud. A rainbow was "upon his head, and his face was as it were the sun, and his feet as pillars of fire" (v. 1). From that description, it must be Jesus.

When seven thunders sounded, John was about to write, but he heard a voice from heaven saying, "Seal up those things which the seven thunders uttered, and write them not" (v. 4). No one knows this secret of the seven thunders. Those things are left for Jesus to reveal in the future.

The angel lifted his hand to heaven and swore by the Creator that there should be "time no longer," or no more delay. That means the second half of the tribulation would come without delay, the first half having been completed.

B. The Mystery of God to Be Finished (10:7)

As soon as the seventh angel blows the trumpet, verse 7 says, the judgment of the seven bowls begins, and the world comes to an end. Thus will the mystery of God be finished as God had declared to His servants the prophets.

Daniel also wrote of a word of mystery:

> Seventy weeks are determined upon thy people and upon thy holy city, to finish the transgression, and to make an end of sins, and to make reconciliation for iniquity, and to bring in everlasting righteousness, and to seal up the vision and prophecy, and to anoint the most Holy (Dan. 9:24).

There are many mysteries that cannot be understood today: Why did God allow Satan to creep into the Garden of Eden? Why did God allow Adam and Eve to fall? Why did sin enter this world? Since these are mysteries of God, we cannot know them now.

When the seventh angel sounds the trumpet, however, the judgment of the seven bowls comes, leading to the end of the world. Then comes the millennial reign of the Lord, during which He will disclose everything plainly.

C. The Little Scroll (10:8-11)

The voice from heaven spoke to John saying, "Go and take the little book [scroll] which is open in the hand of the angel which standeth upon the sea and upon the earth" (v. 8). So John went to the angel and asked for the little scroll. He said to John, "Take it, and eat it up; and it shall make thy belly bitter, but it shall be in thy mouth sweet as honey" (v. 9).

Some people interpret this little scroll to be the scroll sealed with seven seals, but that's wrong. As we have seen, the seven seals have all been opened. What will happen, then, if that scroll is eaten up? Nothing. So what is this scroll? The answer appears in verse 11: "And he said unto me, Thou must prophesy again before many peoples, and nations, and tongues, and kings."

In other words, this little scroll told the things that will happen during the second three and one-half years. In the Old Testament we find similar cases in which the prophet was told to eat a scroll before he received the word of God (see Ezek. 3:1). In the same manner Jesus told John to eat this scroll that he might prophesy.

When John ate the scroll, it was sweet in his mouth. Since it was the Word of God, it was sweeter than honeycomb (see Ps. 19:10). Besides, the prophecy included insight into God's millennial kingdom, followed by a new heaven and a new earth. Therefore the Word was very sweet indeed.

However, the prophecy also told of the Antichrist, who will arise in the form of a beast and run around wildly killing innumerable Jews and others who do not kneel down to him. Hence, for John, it was also a moment of bitterness as he thought of the misery and pain that would be suffered by the people who do not repent during that time.

We turn now to the description of that period in Revelation 11-19. It will be the most tragic and destructive time in human history.

FIVE

THE GREAT TRIBULATION: PART TWO

The second three and one-half years of the tribulation are covered in Revelation 11-19. To understand this period better, let's take a brief overview before getting into the details.

In chapter 11 the period begins, and the seventh angel sounds the trumpet. Chapter 12 is a parenthetical explanation. Chapter 13 is a description of the two beasts, and chapter 14 is a parenthetical prophecy. Chapters 15 and 16 deal with the last woe, started by the last trumpet sound of the seventh angel, the judgment of the seven bowls. Since chapters 12, 13 and 14 are parenthetical, we can better understand the events of the tribulation if we put chapter 15 right after chapter 11.

Chapter 17 deals with the religion of the whore. Chapter 18 describes the downfall of the great city of Babylon. Chapter 19 tells about the advent of Jesus to this earth, bringing the second half of the tribulation period to an end and ushering in the millennial kingdom.

I. THE TRUMPET OF THE SEVENTH ANGEL (11:1-19)

A. Measuring the Temple and Altar and Counting the Worshippers (11:1)

As we move into the second half of the tribulation, the first scene is of John measuring the Jews' temple and altar and counting the worshippers there (see vv. 1-2).

Why such a starting point? In this second part of the tribulation, the Antichrist will fight his life-and-death struggle with the Jews. During the first three and one-half years he was on peaceful terms with them. He aided them and even built the temple for them. However, in the second half of the tribulation, Satan, who was driven out of heaven, enters into the heart of the Antichrist. As a result he breaks the seven-year treaty in the middle and begins a war to annihilate the Jews. Therefore the temple is very significant during that period.

As we saw earlier, the temple was destroyed when Jerusalem fell in A.D. 70. The Jews rose in revolt against the tyranny of Rome, but Jerusalem was besieged and burned by the Roman general Titus. Many instruments made of gold, used for sacrifice in the temple, were burned in this fire, the gold melting into the crevices of the stones. In their search for the hidden gold, the Roman soldiers left no stone unturned, thus fulfilling the prophecy of Jesus in Matthew 24:2.

In the place where the temple previously stood, the Muslims built their own mosque, the Dome of the Rock, between A.D. 687 and 691. Believing it to be the site from which their prophet Mohammed was taken up into heaven, they have made it their second most holy place.

During the Six-Day War of 1967 Israel captured from Jordan the old part of Jerusalem where the mosque stands. Today Israel has finished preparations to rebuild the temple and is ready to start at any time. The money and materials have been collected, and it is the burning desire of the Jews to build a temple there on Mount Moriah.

But the Jews, who cannot even go near the present mosque, will surely start a war with the Muslims when they begin to tear it down to make room for their temple. They will only succeed with the help of a unified Europe.

In the second half of the great tribulation God will try those Jewish people with fire who do not believe in Jesus Christ, choosing rather to reject Him. After that God will measure the sincerity of their faith. He will shelter those who worship Him in the temple and at the altar, according to the measure of their faith; others (those who are outside the temple) He will cast away.

Among the Jews today are pious people who fervently worship the Lord through Judaism. But there are also others who ridicule Judaism, denying the existence of God. In order to separate those two types of people, John measured the temple and the altar and counted the worshippers with a rod-like reed.

B. The Outer Court (11:2)

However, the Lord told John not to measure the court outside the temple (see v. 2). That means God will save only those pious worshippers inside the temple. As for those on the outside, in the temple court, God will abandon them into the hands of the Antichrist for forty-two months, whether they are Jews or gentiles.

The Antichrist has been making preparation for his rule of the world in the first three and one-half years. Now he will change his shape into a beast and for the following three and one-half years rule the world with full authority. He will break the seven-year treaty he had made with Israel and set up his own idol-image in the altar of the temple, forcing the Jews to worship it. This is foretold in Daniel 9:27:

> And he shall confirm the covenant with many for one week: and in the midst of the week he shall cause the sacrifice and the oblation to cease, and for the overspreading of abominations he shall make it desolate, even until the consummation, and that determined shall be poured upon the desolate.

This is also the time of which our Lord warned:

> When ye therefore shall see the abomination of desolation, spoken of by Daniel the prophet, stand in the holy place, (whoso readeth, let him understand:) Then let them which be in Judea flee into the mountains (Matt. 24:15-16).

Since devout Jews will worship only God, not idols, they will, of course, resist. Inevitably, a bloody massacre will ensue. The Bible predicted this, calling it the tribulation of Jacob: "Alas! for that day is great, so that none is like it: it is even the time of Jacob's trouble; but he shall be saved out of it" (Jer. 30:7).

After measuring the temple and altar and counting those who worship there, God will move everyone obedient to His will to the shelter. This scene soon appears.

C. The Two Witnesses (11:3-13)

Two witnesses, clothed in sackcloth, appear and will prophesy 1,260 days. That's three and one-half years when the month is counted as 30 days — the second part of the tribulation. The 144,000 Jews sealed by God on their foreheads to be preachers are seen no more; they have been taken up into heaven, where they praise God. Now it is time for the two witnesses to come and prophesy.

Of what will they testify? First, they will proclaim that people receive salvation by faith in Jesus Christ through the precious blood of the cross. Second, they will testify that the Antichrist is not the messiah but a wicked criminal, the son of perdition. Third, they will bear witness of the imminent judgment of God. How the Antichrist will hate these two witnesses! He will grind his teeth with vexation, taking revenge by killing them.

Who do you think the two witnesses are? The Bible says, "These are the two olive trees, and the two candlesticks" (v. 4). They were seen by the prophet Zechariah about five hundred years before Christ (see Zech. 4:1-14). When Zechariah asked the angel the meaning of the two olive trees, he was told, "These are the two anointed ones, that stand by the Lord of the whole earth" (Zech. 4:14). Thus, the two olive trees have already been worshipping God in heaven for more than twenty-five hundred years. The two witnesses were Moses and Elijah, who comforted Jesus on the Mount of Transfiguration (see Luke 9:28-31).

When the Israelites became depraved and worshipped idols during the time of King Ahab, Elijah prayed to God that it might not rain, and God shut the door of heaven for three and one-half years. In the second half of the tribulation the two olive trees will also shut the door of heaven, and it will not rain (see v. 6).

When Moses led the Israelites out of Egypt, God first

gave him ten plagues to persuade Pharaoh to release the people. One of these plagues was to change the water of the Nile River into blood. During the second half of the tribulation, the two olive trees will strike the earth with the same plague (see v. 6).

The witnesses will return to this world in the flesh and preach about Jesus. The Bible says Elijah did not see death but was caught up into heaven riding a fiery chariot driven by fiery horses (see 2 Kin. 2:1-11). Although it was known that Moses climbed Mount Nebo to die, his body was never found. The Bible says that Michael the archangel contended with the devil for Moses' body (see Jude 9). Because God buried Moses' body, no one was able to find his grave (see Deut. 34:5-6). God hid Moses' body so that He could use him again for His purpose at the end of the world.

Therefore the two olive trees and two candlesticks are unmistakably Moses and Elijah. God sends them again in the flesh to this world to witness of Jesus Christ, showing His love and mercy in order to deliver one more soul from hell.

If anyone tries to hurt the two witnesses while they're prophesying, "fire proceedeth out of their mouth, and devoureth their enemies" (v. 5). (Once, when Elijah was on the top of a hill, two bands of soldiers who came to seize him were consumed by fire which fell from heaven; see 2 Kings 1:9-12). Thus, while these two witnesses are prophesying, no one can hurt them, and the Antichrist is in constant agony until the second three and one-half years are almost over. Finally, he rises to oppose them.

By this time the two witnesses will have fulfilled their mission. Then the beast that has come up from the bottomless pit, the Antichrist, will kill them (see v. 7). The preacher of Christ's gospel will never die before God's appointed time.

The Antichrist then throws their bodies into the streets

of Jerusalem, spiritually called Sodom and Egypt, because it is the adulterous city opposing God by setting up an idol of the Antichrist (see v. 8).

All the world's people congratulate themselves for the death of the two witnesses and refuse to let their bodies be placed in a tomb (see v. 9). The people send gifts one to another and make merry. The two witnesses had harshly rebuked them and brought a judgment of drought because of their wickedness, so it is with great joy that they celebrate their deaths (see v. 10).

However, "after three days and an half the Spirit of life from God entered into them, and they stood upon their feet." Then a loud voice from heaven speaks: "Come up hither." They ascend to heaven before everyone's eyes, causing everyone to be very frightened (see vv. 11-12).

At the same time, a great earthquake strikes, and a tenth of the city falls, killing seven thousand people. After witnessing such a dreadful scene, the remaining people temporarily give glory to God (see v. 13).

D. The Trumpet of the Seventh Angel (11:14-18)

Then the sound of a trumpet by the seventh angel was heard. This is the last in the series of trumpets by the seven angels who appeared when the scroll's seventh seal was opened by Jesus.

When the trumpet of the seventh angel sounded, John heard the proclamation to take over the world: "And the seventh angel sounded; and there were great voices in heaven, saying, 'The kingdoms of this world are become the kingdoms of our Lord, and of his Christ; and he shall reign for ever and ever' " (11:15).

As we have seen, the second three and one-half years of the tribulation were almost finished when the two witnesses died. This is prior to the war of Armageddon.

Now that Jesus has regained this world, which had been under the power of Satan, He takes it over. All the procedures to redeem creation have been completed.

As soon as the twenty-four elders, sitting on the thrones, heard the trumpet, they became overwhelmed with joy, fell on their faces and worshipped God. They sang this song of praise:

> We give thee thanks, O Lord God Almighty, which art, and wast, and art to come; because thou hast taken to thee thy great power, and hast reigned. And the nations were angry, and thy wrath is come, and the time of the dead, that they should be judged, and that thou shouldest give reward unto thy servants the prophets, and to the saints, and them that fear thy name, small and great; and shouldest destroy them which destroy the earth (11:17-18).

In that song the elders foresee the end of the tribulation; the millennial kingdom; the general resurrection of all the dead along with the final judgment of Him who sits on the throne; and the coming of a new heaven and a new earth.

Because the gleaning of salvation is come to an end when the two witnesses are taken into heaven, this world will be practically finished.

II. THE ARK OF THE TESTAMENT IN THE TEMPLE (11:19)

When the elders finished praising God, the temple of God was opened in heaven, and John saw the ark of the testament accompanied by lightning, voices, thunderings, an earthquake and great hail.

The temple was not opened at regular times. It was

opened only once a year when the high priest entered to offer sacrifices.

What does it mean, then, that the temple was opened and the ark of the covenant was seen? Although mankind sinned and fell, God promised that He would forgive our sins, save us and make a new world for us. By opening the temple, God was confirming that promise.

But after God's assurance of His promise comes a foreboding of the last judgment in the lightning, voices, thunderings, earthquake and great hail. The world is rushing headlong toward its end during the second half of the tribulation.

III. PARENTHETICAL EXPLANATION OF THE FATE OF ISRAEL (12:1-17)

Revelation 12 explains in detail what the fate of Israel will be during the second part of the tribulation. As I have mentioned several times, this occurs when the Antichrist breaks his seven-year treaty with Israel and sets up his own image in the temple of God, forcing the Jews to worship it. Since they are monotheistic, they strongly resist this demand and suffer for it. If we study chapter 12 with that in mind, we'll understand it better.

A. A Great Wonder in Heaven (12:1-2)

Who was this woman clothed with the sun? Some say she represents the church. However, the Bible never uses the image of a woman to symbolize the church. The church is the virgin engaged to Christ, not a woman about to deliver a child. But there is a nation that was called "the woman" in the Bible: "Sing, O barren, thou that didst not bear; break forth into singing, and cry aloud, thou that didst not travail with child: for more are the children of the desolate than the children of the married wife, saith the Lord" (Is. 54:1).

Along with this passage, let's also look at the book of Hosea, which calls Israel the wife who fled from her husband. Israel was sometimes called a married woman when she was obedient to God. At other times, when she disobeyed God, she was called a divorced woman or a widow. Thus, Israel was always compared to a woman rather than a virgin.

Further, in Genesis 37:9-10, Joseph, one of the twelve sons of Israel (Jacob), dreamed a dream. In that dream "the sun and the moon and the eleven stars" bowed down to Joseph. That meant that Joseph's father and mother, along with his eleven brothers, would bow down to him. In this dream the sun represented Israel. From these two examples we can deduce that the image of the woman in Revelation 12 represents Israel.

Verse 2 says that birth pangs came upon the woman. That does not mean Israel will deliver something in tribulation. Revelation 12 is a parenthetical, historical explanation of why the devil hates Israel so much and the Antichrist tries to annihilate it.

B. Another Wonder in Heaven (12:3-5)

The son delivered in verse 5 was Jesus Christ. He was not an ordinary man but One who would rule the nations with an iron rod: "I will declare the decree: the Lord hath said unto me, Thou art my Son; this day have I begotten thee.... Thou shalt break them with a rod of iron; thou shalt dash them in pieces like a potter's vessel" (Ps. 2:7,9).

The red dragon was about to devour the son of the woman. In studying the life of Jesus, we find that the devil followed Jesus constantly, watching for an opportunity to destroy Him. For example, when Jesus was born, King Herod tried to use the Magi to locate the baby so he could kill Him. No doubt inspired by Satan, Herod gave orders to kill all the boys in and around Bethlehem who were two years old and under when his ploy failed (see Matt. 2:1-18). In Bethlehem the tomb still remains where the massacred babies were buried together.

Finally, Satan had Jesus crucified. However, He was resurrected and ascended into heaven, now sitting at the right hand of God. That's why Revelation 12:5 says, "Her child was caught up unto God, and to his throne."

Who is this "another wonder in heaven," the great red dragon? He is a murderer who is called the old serpent, the devil, Satan or Lucifer. He was one of the cherubim called "the anointed cherub that covereth" (Ezek. 28:14). He was also one of the archangels, the highest rank in the hierarchy of angels, but he became proud (see Is. 14:13-14; Ezek. 28:17). This eventually drove him to compete with God (see Rev. 12:7). As a result he was driven out of heaven (see vv. 8-9) and now rules the power of the air (see Eph. 2:2), located between the heavenly throne and the earth.

In the book of Genesis, when God created heaven and earth and all things in them, He saw that it was all good except for one place: the firmament in the midst of the waters (see Gen. 1:6-8). The phrase "it was good" is omitted in the account of that place, and I believe it's because it was occupied by the devil and the other evil spirits who opposed God.

Revelation 12 says Lucifer drew a third part of the stars of heaven with his tail and cast them to the earth (v. 4). That signifies he incited a third of the angels to join him when he fell, starting the history of rebellion on the earth. We can be thankful, however, that two-thirds of the angels did *not* fall. Therefore when one demon attacks us, two angels of God are available to protect us.

Verse 3 describes the red dragon as having seven heads and ten horns. That shows he will oppose God to the end of the world, a point further explained in Revelation 13.

The seven heads represent the seven nations God raised up that most violently opposed Him: Assyria, Babylon, Media and Persia, Egypt, Greece, Rome and the Antichrist's country that will be restored. The devil has gone all out to destroy God's people through those seven heads.

The ten horns of this dragon signify the ten countries of unified Europe that will be formed in the early part of the tribulation. Through that union Satan will make his final struggle not to be cast away from the earth.

In Genesis 3:15, however, God declared that Jesus Christ, the seed of woman, would crush the devil's head.

From the time Lucifer heard that word of prophecy, he has exerted all his effort to prevent "the seed of woman" from being born, and thus began humanity's bloody history of constant war and murder. Cain was disobedient to God, but Abel was obedient. Therefore the devil inspired Cain to murder Abel, for he (Satan) was afraid the Messiah might be born from Abel. First John 3:12 clearly says, "Not as Cain, who was of that wicked one, and slew his brother...." In other words, Cain killed Abel at the instigation of the devil (see Gen. 4:1-8).

Later, when the whole world was judged for its wickedness, Noah found favor in the sight of the Lord (see Gen. 6:8-9). Then the devil feared the Messiah would come out of the descendants of Noah, so he caused Noah to become drunk (see Gen. 9:20-21) and his offspring to be depraved. As a result, they fell into a snare. They gathered themselves in the land of Shinar and built the tower of Babel in rebellion against God (see Gen. 11:1-4). This was also done at the instigation of the devil.

Afterward, God chose to make a nation out of Abraham's offspring to carry out His will, but the devil again interfered, fearing the Messiah would come out of his seed. In Egypt he tried to exterminate the people of Israel through Pharaoh (see the book of Exodus).

When the Israelites, led by Joshua, came to the land of

Canaan and settled there, Satan repeatedly corrupted them through idolatry, for he was afraid the Messiah might come from them. Therefore, the Israelites were destroyed by Assyria and Persia and carried away as captives.

Through the grace of God, however, many Israelites returned from captivity. This time the devil incited them to kill Jesus. But once more God thwarted him by raising Jesus on the third day.

C. The Woman Who Fled Into the Wilderness (12:6)

Because the red dragon had been repeatedly frustrated in attempting to swallow the child throughout the long history of the world, he became furious and hated the woman who gave birth to the child — namely Israel. Therefore the history of Israel has been a succession of ordeals and sufferings.

Since Christ ascended into heaven, Satan has wreaked his vengeance through many Jew-haters, most notably Hitler and the communists in the Soviet Union. During the second half of the tribulation he will launch an unprecedented extermination campaign against the Jews.

Verse 6 says, "The woman fled into the wilderness, where she hath a place prepared of God, that they should feed her there a thousand two hundred and threescore days." That means God will make a refuge for Israel from the persecution of the Antichrist for 1,260 days, or three and one-half years.

Where is this shelter? The place is revealed in the book of Isaiah. Several Christian groups from the United States have flown airplane loads of Bibles and canned food there, hiding the material under the earth and between the rocks in preparation for the time when Israel will take shelter there. Isn't that a wonderful thing God did by moving the hearts of the people? He spoke of the time of Israel's need for such protection in Isaiah 26:20-27:1:

> Come, my people, enter thou into thy chambers, and shut thy doors about thee: hide thyself as it were for a little moment, until the indignation be overpast. For, behold, the Lord cometh out of his place to punish the inhabitants of the earth for their iniquity: the earth also shall disclose her blood, and shall no more cover her slain. In that day the Lord with his sore and great and strong sword shall punish leviathan the piercing serpent, even leviathan that crooked serpent; and he shall slay the dragon that is in the sea.

Mark that scripture, for there God clearly said He will hide the Israelites from the rage of the Antichrist. The passage is preceded by a verse telling about those who believe in Jesus Christ: "Thy dead men shall live, together with my dead body shall they arise. Awake and sing, ye that dwell in dust: for thy dew is as the dew of herbs, and the earth shall cast out the dead" (Is. 26:19).

The dead of the Lord shall rise again and ascend into heaven first, and then the Israelites will hide themselves in the secret chamber. Long ago Isaiah predicted all this accurately. Now look at the place where Israel will hide.

> For it shall be, that, as a wandering bird cast out of the nest, so the daughters of Moab shall be at the fords of Arnon. Take counsel, execute judgment; make thy shadow as the night in the midst of the noonday; hide the outcasts; betray not him that wandereth. Let mine outcasts dwell with thee, Moab; be thou a covert to them from the

116

face of the spoiler (Is. 16:2-4).

Here "the spoiler" signifies the Antichrist. When he launches his invasion, the land of Moab becomes God's hiding place for Israel.

When the Israelites first crossed the Jordan River and entered the land of Canaan, God ordered them to build cities of refuge on both sides of the river so that a person who had accidentally killed someone might flee there to safety (see Num. 35:9-15). Those cities symbolize the place where Israel will take shelter during the tribulation.

Where is Moab located? When I visited Israel some years ago, I went there. Roughly speaking, Moab corresponds to the present highlands of Transjordan. About an hour's ride on the highway from Jerusalem will bring you to the highlands of Transjordan. Once there, you will meet only the blazing sun and swirling gusts of sand.

In the midst of that desert, however, is the strongest fortress in the world. The name of it is Petra. It was discovered in the nineteenth century and is situated between steep mountains. The only entrance is through a narrow, twisting canyon. It is not accessible to tanks, nor can airplanes attack it directly, because the mountains are so precipitous. With the buildings all cut into the rock cliffs, Petra is a formidable fortress. Theologians generally agree that Israel's hiding place during the second half of the tribulation will be Petra, in the highlands of Transjordan.

D. The War in Heaven (12:7-12)

According to verse 7, there is war in heaven, a cosmic conflict fought between Michael, the prince of the divine host, and the dragon. The time has come when the antagonistic dragon should be cast out, as all his power was brought to an end when Jesus opened the last seal.

As foretold in Isaiah 24:21, God will punish "the host of the high ones that are on high" — in other words, the red dragon that deceives the whole world. God will punish the kings of the Antichrist; and when He goes to Jerusalem and stands there, the sun will be ashamed and the moon will be confounded, and the Lord will be glorified before the saints who are saved.

In that final, intense conflict in heaven between Michael and the dragon, Satan is driven out of heaven because he is not equal to the archangel: "And the great dragon was cast out, that old serpent, called the Devil, and Satan, which deceiveth the whole world: he was cast out into the earth, and his angels were cast out with him" (v. 9).

When the devil is cast out, a great voice in heaven says, "The accuser of our brethren is cast down, which accused them before our God day and night. And they overcame him by the blood of the Lamb, and by the word of their testimony; and they loved not their lives unto the death" (vv. 10-11).

Satan still accuses us before God. But we overcome his unceasing accusations by claiming the blood of Christ and the forgiveness it affords.

A church that is under the influence of the devil offers no songs or sermons praising the precious blood of Jesus Christ. However, if a church is full of songs and sermons praising His precious blood, the Holy Spirit will be at work there.

Today modernists, or "new theologians," argue that Jesus Christ died not as Savior but as a great teacher or a great leader, so His death was self-immolation. This is the voice of the devil. "Therefore rejoice, ye heavens, and ye that dwell in them. Woe to the inhabitants of the earth and of the sea! for the devil is come down unto you, having great wrath, because he knoweth that he hath but a short time" (12:12).

By that time we shall be in heaven, but those remaining on the earth will be hurt by the rage of the devil, who will recklessly attack anyone crossing his path, knowing his time is short.

E. The Refuge of the Woman and the Remnants (12:13-17)

Being thus driven to the earth, the dragon begins to persecute the woman, the mother of the male child, or Christ, who has brought such a fatal blow to him. His intention is to take his final revenge on Israel. The fate of Israel is indeed miserable. If they had believed in Jesus, such a tragedy would have been avoided. However, they did not accept Him, so they must pass through this ordeal at the end of the world.

Then verse 14 says that "to the woman were given two wings of a great eagle, that she might fly into the wilderness, into her place, where she is nourished for a time, and times, and half a time, from the face of the serpent." This is why Jesus said:

> Then let them which be in Judea flee into the mountains: let him which is on the housetop not come down to take any thing out of his house: neither let him which is in the field return back to take his clothes. And woe unto them that are with child, and to them that give suck in those days! But pray ye that your flight be not in the winter, neither on the sabbath day: for then shall be great tribulation, such as was not since the beginning of the world to this time, no, nor ever shall be (Matt. 24:16-21).

Through this scripture Jesus was showing how severe

119

the situation of that time will be. When the Antichrist gives the stern order for all Jews to be put to death, they will flee to Petra without looking back.

The Bible says the woman, or Israel, flew into her place. However, there is no airport in Petra, and it would be impossible for a helicopter to transport such a large company of people to escape the carnage. So how could they go? The Lord will provide a way. In the New Testament we find a miracle that can solve the problem.

Obeying the command of God, Philip went "south unto the way that goeth down from Jerusalem unto Gaza, which is desert" (Acts 8:26, see vv. 26-40). On his way he met an Ethiopian eunuch. Philip preached Jesus to him and baptized him in water. When they came up out of the water, the Holy Spirit suddenly took Philip away and put him down at Azotus, a city about one hundred miles from Gaza. Thus, when Philip came up out of the water and walked one step, he was transported to a place one hundred miles away.

When the Jews flee from the Antichrist, they cannot go to Petra unless they're helped by a miracle of God. The army of the Antichrist will run after them with tanks and vehicles. The Jews, running on foot, would soon be overtaken and killed unless they fly with "the wings of a great eagle" as predicted in the Bible.

The Jews take refuge at Petra and are nourished there "for a time, and times, and half a time" (v. 14) — the second three and one-half years of the tribulation. The flood of water Satan casts after Israel (see v. 15) symbolizes the multitude of people in the Antichrist's army that will charge at Petra.

Then verse 16 says "the earth helped the woman, and the earth opened her mouth, and swallowed up the flood which the dragon cast out of his mouth." The earth's opening her mouth means an earthquake takes place. As the army of the Antichrist approaches Petra, a strong earthquake causes deep cracks in the earth's surface that swallow the army. Several avenues of attack are tried, but every time the armies are engulfed by a chasm in the earth. The day is not far away when all these things will happen.

"The dragon was wroth with the woman, and went to make war with the remnant of her seed, which keep the commandments of God, and have the testimony of Jesus Christ" (v. 17). The Jews who believed in Jesus were transported by God to Petra. The remaining Jews are all secular, yet they also keep the commandment of God and do not worship the Antichrist's image. Besides, some gentiles believe in Jesus belatedly. The dragon now stands ready to make war on those people.

Thus, the Jews and all the Christians are killed during the second half of the tribulation. No one can escape from this annihilation, except those in Petra. Even the two witnesses are killed.

IV. ONE BEAST AND ANOTHER BEAST (13:1-18)

A. The Beast Out of the Sea; Comparison to Daniel's Vision (13:1)

John "saw a beast rise up out of the sea." The sea here signifies the multitude of people. The specific body of water John saw is the Mediterranean Sea. This verse means that a beast will come out of the coastal region of the Mediterranean Sea — in other words, out of the former territory of the Roman empire. In the vision of God, beasts represent the kings of the earth. Accordingly, the beast that rises out of the sea signifies the Antichrist who rises out of the large crowd of restored Rome.

To understand this beast better, we must first know about the image seen by the Babylonian king Nebuchadnezzar and described in the book of Daniel.

1. The Image Nebuchadnezzar Saw in His Dream

In Daniel 2 we read that King Nebuchadnezzar dreamed a troubling dream in about 606 B.C. In it he saw a great image that had the form of a man. God was prophesying human history through this dream, and Daniel provided the interpretation (see Dan. 2:31-45).

The image Nebuchadnezzar saw had a head, breast, arms, belly and thighs, legs and feet. Suddenly a "stone was cut out without hands" and hit the image, breaking it to pieces; and the stone that smote the image filled the whole earth (Dan. 2:34-35). That was the vision Nebuchadnezzar saw. Then Daniel gave the following detailed interpretation.

The head made of fine gold. This represents the neo-Babylonian empire, which conquered the southern Jewish kingdom of Judah and lasted until 583 B.C. As an absolute monarchy, it had absolute political power like gold, but it was conquered by the Medo-Persian empire.

The breast and the arms. The two silver arms represent a united empire made of two kingdoms. That was the Medo-Persian empire, whose army, under a king named Cyrus, conquered Babylon in 583 B.C.

Media and Persia ruled the empire alternately until 380 B.C. Because its political system was not purely despotic, it was weaker than the neo-Babylonian empire. However, since silver is stronger than gold, it was stronger militarily in spite of its weaker political system.

The belly and the thighs. The belly and thighs of brass signify Greece. Brass is stronger than silver, and Alexander the Great of Greece vanquished the Medo-Persian empire in 380 B.C. By 323 B.C. he had brought all the known territory of Europe under his control.

Two legs. Following the death of Alexander the Great,

the Greek empire was divided into four parts; they were unified by Rome in 30 B.C. The Roman empire is represented by the legs of iron. Just as iron is stronger than brass, so Rome was far stronger than Greece.

By A.D. 364 Rome had conquered all the known world. In 364, however, it was divided in half by religious conflict. The empire in the east was united under the banner of what we know today as the Greek Orthodox Church. The empire in the west flew the banner of the church centered in Rome. Eventually the split empire fell.

Ten toes. Afterward comes the age of ten toes and the description of the image in the form of a man. This signifies that the church age would rise in the territory of the Roman empire. Finally, the age of the ten toes will come.

Ten toes mean that ten kingdoms will be united. The feet were made partly of iron and partly of clay. That signifies the coalition of nations with totally different political structures. The "strong" structure is absolute monarchy, and the "weak" structure is democracy. The two will be mixed to form one country — a unified Europe. This coalition will come together soon.

A stone cut out without hands. "A stone was cut out without hands" (Dan. 2:34) and struck the image, breaking it to pieces. That stone then became a great mountain and filled the whole earth (Dan. 2:35). Jesus Christ is that stone.

The interpretation is that Jesus will come again and destroy unified Europe, and all the nations in the world will belong to Him.

2. Daniel's Dream of Four Beasts

God also showed Daniel a vision that he recorded in chapter 7 of his book. In 555 B.C. Daniel had a dream in which he saw four beasts. Through these beasts God was showing Daniel future things of the world. These beasts were predators that bit and tore at each other.

A lion that had eagle's wings. The first beast was like a lion but had the wings of an eagle (see Dan. 7:4). Before long, however, the wings were plucked, and it stood erect like a man and spoke. This beast represented King Nebuchadnezzar and showed he would unify and rule the empire as swiftly as a lion or an eagle.

The vision also referred to Nebuchadnezzar's becoming insane and living in the fields as punishment for his pride with the wild beasts. However, when he repented of his sin, God restored him, and a man's heart was given to him (see Dan. 4:24-37).

A bear that had three ribs between its teeth. The second beast Daniel saw was a bear raised up on one side, with three ribs in its mouth between its teeth (see Dan. 7:5). This bear signified the Medo-Persian empire.

The statement that the bear was raised on one side means that in the coalition of Media and Persia, Persia was the stronger. This empire was represented by a bear because it had the characteristics of a bear — it was strong but clumsy as it rushed recklessly with its military might. Its army did not win in war through great strategy but by overpowering the enemy with enormous numbers of soldiers. Xerxes of Persia, for example, mobilized a force of five million in his expedition to Greece. Half the men were in the regular army, and the rest were engaged in the supply area.

Lydia, Babylon and Egypt fought as allies against the Medo-Persian empire and were defeated. The three ribs the bear had between its teeth signify those three nations.

A leopard that had four heads and four wings. After the clumsy bear passed, Daniel saw a leopard with four heads and four wings (see Dan. 7:6). A leopard is a swift animal, and the leopard with wings meant that it would conquer the whole world with lightning swiftness. This was a reference to Greece under Alexander the Great.

The four heads of the leopard signified Alexander's four generals. After his death, the empire was divided among those generals. The four parts were Thrace, Macedonia, Syria and Egypt.

An exceedingly strong beast. The fourth beast Daniel saw was dreadful and exceedingly strong, with great iron teeth. It devoured and broke into pieces, and it "stamped the residue with the feet of it" (Dan. 7:7). This beast represented the Roman empire. By 30 B.C. Rome subdued Thrace, Macedonia, Syria and Egypt, bringing all of civilized Europe under its control. It was the most extensive empire in world history.

This beast had ten horns, which correspond to the ten toes of the image in Nebuchadnezzar's dream. As Daniel was looking, a little horn came up out of the ten horns and plucked three of the first horns by the roots. This little horn signifies the Antichrist, who will appear and dictate to the whole world, opposing God and causing pain to the saints for three and one-half years before God destroys him.

B. The Beast John Saw (13:1-2)

If we compare the image and the beasts in the book of Daniel with the beast out of the sea in Revelation 13, we can better understand the meaning. John's beast also had ten horns and seven heads and represented the Antichrist, who will appear in the age of the ten toes at the end of history.

1. The Ten Horns That Wear Ten Crowns

The ten horns wearing crowns signify the rulers of the ten nations in Europe. In other words, ten nations in

Europe will arise in the former territory of the ancient Roman empire. Watch closely the political development of Europe, keeping in mind that unified Europe will grow out of ten countries.

2. The Seven Heads

The beast had seven heads, and on each of them was a blasphemous name. The seven heads with blasphemous names represent seven kingdoms that oppose God and persecute His people.

The fact that seven heads belong to one body shows us that it is made up of parts of six kingdoms and one present kingdom that opposed God. Revelation 17:10 says there are seven kings; "five are fallen, and one is, and the other is not yet come." It will be explained further in Revelation 17.

3. The Characteristics of the Beast

The beast that came out of the sea looked like a mixture of three beasts. First, it is said to be like a leopard, which represents the swiftness of ancient Greece. Second, it has the feet of a bear, which means it will possess a large army like the Medo-Persian empire. Third, it has the mouth of a lion, which means it possesses mighty power like that of ancient Babylon, so as to conquer the whole world.

Altogether, this beast symbolizes revived Rome, the union of ten European countries that will become the strongest nation in human history.

4. The Dragon and the Antichrist

Verse 2 says the dragon gave the beast his power, his throne and great authority. This is the same dragon that was cast out of heaven after he was defeated in his fight with Michael, at the end of the first three and one-half years of the tribulation. When he comes to earth, he gives his power, his throne and great authority to the Antichrist, hoping he can win in his stead, much as parents anchor their hopes in their children.

C. The Revival of the Head Fatally Wounded (13:3-4)

One of the beast's heads becomes fatally wounded, a prediction that the Antichrist will be killed. Imagine the Antichrist being stabbed to death by a terrorist. As preparations are made for his funeral, suddenly his deadly wound is healed miraculously! He is revived by the power of the devil.

The whole world wonders at such a miracle. The news media around the world had reported the death of the head of the state of united Europe, and the date of his funeral was set. But then all the media suddenly report he has been revived. Wouldn't people be amazed? Suppose that John F. Kennedy, after he was reported to have died, had been revived. The journalists of the world would have talked about it for weeks, and people all over the world would have admired him, thinking him an extraordinary person.

Besides wondering at the resuscitation of the Antichrist, people everywhere will worship him and the dragon. Pooling their strength, the dragon and the beast will mobilize enormous political, economic and military power. People will say, "Who is like unto the beast? who is able to make war with him?" (v. 4).

Since the dragon is Satan, the beast will probably make an insignia of a dragon. Dragons represent evil in the West, but in the East they are revered and worshipped. Koreans and Chinese call a throne the seat of a dragon; the face of a king, the face of a dragon; and if anyone sees a dragon in his dream, the interpretation is that the person will have a lucky day. (For many years in the Orient, the devil had the stage all to himself because the region had been outside the influence of Christianity.)

People will probably be compelled by the Antichrist to make insignias of the dragon for the purpose of dragon worship. The world will soon be covered with portraits of dragons everywhere: the flag of the dragon, the insignia of the dragon and the statue of the dragon. Afterward the Antichrist will also be worshipped.

D. Outrage of the Beast (13:5-10)

The Antichrist will trample the world, wielding great power for the second half of the tribulation (see v. 5). Not knowing his true status, however, he will be proud and utter blasphemy, publicly denouncing heaven and those who are there (see v. 6). When he delivers an address over the radio, or when he has a press conference, he will always begin by saying blasphemous words or denouncing the saints in heaven.

Furthermore, he will war against Jewish Christians for forty-two months, ordering them to be killed wherever they are found. But they will be hiding during that time in the fortress of Petra.

Everyone whose name is not written in the Lamb's book of life will bow down to the beast, regardless of age, sex, possession and rank (see v. 8). So verse 10 says that the patience and faith of the saints are needed to the end.

John encourages us, however, with the prophecy that "he that leadeth into captivity shall go into captivity" (v. 10). The Antichrist will go into captivity himself, and with the sword with which many Jews were killed, he also will be killed. Knowing this, we should persevere to the end.

E. The Other Beast Which Came Out of the Earth (13:11-18)

In verse 11 John "beheld another beast coming up out of the earth; and he had two horns like a lamb, and he spake as a dragon."

Notice that this false prophet will mimic Jesus the Lamb. He, however, has only two horns, whereas Jesus has seven. And whereas the Holy Spirit preaches Jesus Christ with all His might, doing honor to Him, so the false prophet will try desperately to do honor to the Antichrist.

Further, the false prophet will exercise the power of the Antichrist and publicize his name (see v. 12). The Holy Spirit is entrusted with authority given by Jesus Christ and acts in His name. The false prophet makes the earth and its inhabitants worship the Antichrist. The Holy Spirit leads us to worship Jesus Christ. The false prophet will also do great wonders before the Antichrist and all the people:

> And he doeth great wonders, so that he maketh fire come down from heaven on the earth in the sight of men, and deceiveth them that dwell on the earth by the means of those miracles which he had power to do in the sight of the beast; saying to them that dwell on the earth, that they should make an image to the beast, which had the wound by a sword, and did live (vv. 13-14).

The false prophet has the people make an idol of the Antichrist and gives life to it so it can speak (see v. 15). From a scientific standpoint, that is now easy to do, since electronic devices could be installed to make the image appear to speak. However the idol gained speech, it seemed to John as though life had been given to it.

The false prophet then makes everyone worship the

idol, and those who do not are killed. It's a ghastly thought.

As the 144,000 preachers of God were sealed on their foreheads, so the false prophet next causes all the people who are under the reign of the Antichrist to receive a mark on their right hand or forehead. He forbids those without this mark to engage in any kind of commercial activities. In other words, they starve to death because they can't make a living or buy food (see vv. 16-17).

In verse 18 the name of the Antichrist is represented by a number, which is 666. This is a satanic number: the number of the dragon is six, the number of the Antichrist is six and the number of the false prophet is also six. Hence, it represents the evil trinity of wickedness.

The triune God could be represented by the number 777, since seven is the biblical number of completion or perfection.

Thus, those evil ones parody the divine trinity of God. The dragon corresponds to the Father; the Antichrist corresponds to the Son; and the false prophet corresponds to the Holy Spirit. As God the Father gives all His power to Jesus, and the Holy Spirit does honor to Jesus, so the dragon gives all his power to the Antichrist, and the false prophet does honor to the Antichrist.

V. PARENTHETICAL PROPHECY (14:1-20)

As a parenthetical prophecy, Revelation 14 shows things that will happen during the second half of the tribulation. A more detailed interpretation will follow in chapter 15.

A. 144,000 After the First Three and One-half Years (14:1-5)

Since the beginning of the second three and one-half

years, we have seen no more mention of the 144,000 Jewish preachers who propagated the gospel during the first part of the tribulation. Now we find them on Mount Zion in heaven, singing a new song no one else could learn (see vv. 1, 3).

Why could nobody else learn this song? Because those particular evangelists have endured and overcome the severe trials of the first half of the tribulation, and those who have not cannot sing the new song.

Verse 4 says they were not defiled with women, which means they did not bow down to the idols. It is spiritual fornication to love the world and worship idols. The verse also says they are chaste, and the Greek word used means "celibate." Hence, the 144,000 are all married faithfully to the Lamb, and they totally obey His guidance. They are the firstfruits of the Jews in the tribulation.

B. The Angel's Proclamation of the Gospel (14:6-7)

John next saw an angel's proclamation of the gospel. Preaching the gospel is not usually a task assigned to angels. The angel who appeared to Cornelius, for example, did not preach the gospel himself but told Cornelius to call Peter and hear it from him (see Acts 10:1-8).

The angel's message was a mixture of hope and warning: "Fear God, and give glory to him; for the hour of his judgment is come: and worship him that made heaven, and earth, and the sea, and the fountains of waters" (v. 7).

God was giving those left on earth another chance to respond to the preaching of the gospel from the 144,000 preachers, Moses and Elijah.

C. The Falling Down of
   Babylon the Great (14:8)

Following the first angel's preaching of the eternal gospel, the second angel predicted that Babylon the great, which has always rebelled against God, would fall.

Though it is not certain where the Antichrist will make the capital of his kingdom, the city he chooses will become the central city in the world. It is foretold, however, that God will destroy it during the second half of the tribulation. Thus, Revelation 14 is a parenthetical prophecy and will begin to be fulfilled in chapter 15.

D. The Warning of the
   Third Angel (14:9-11)

The third angel followed and said, "If any man worship the beast and his image, and receive his mark in his forehead, or in his hand...he shall be tormented with fire and brimstone in the presence of the holy angels, and in the presence of the Lamb" (vv. 9-10). The most dreadful judgment is to be cast into the lake burning with fire and brimstone. Those who do not believe in Jesus now, however, die and go to hell, which is different from the lake of fire and brimstone.

Hell is the place where souls apart from Christ gather together after the death of the body. It is a place of torment. Luke 16 tells us of the rich man who went to hell and saw Lazarus, who was in the bosom of Abraham. The rich man appeals to Abraham to send Lazarus with a bit of water to cool his tongue. If hell is so painful, how great must be the pain when one is later cast into the lake burning with fire and brimstone!

Those who worship the beast and his image and receive his mark in their forehead or hand will be cast into this lake. The word is *Gehenna* in the Greek and was called the Valley of the Children of Hinnom in the Old Testament. This valley was a common dump where all the trash of Jerusalem was burned.

At that time, however, human beings will be piled up and burned — those who worshipped the beast and his image and had his number on their foreheads or hands.

Jehovah's Witnesses argue that when people die, their souls also die with them. However, verse 11 says that the souls cast into the lake burning with fire and brimstone will be eternally tormented, and the smoke ascends forever and ever.

People doubt whether there are really such places as heaven and hell. The Bible clearly states these places exist. All the prophecies of the Bible are being fulfilled. Why, then, would this scripture not be fulfilled? That's why Jesus commented on the soul of the man who betrayed him, "It had been good for that man if he had not been born" (Matt. 26:24). Jesus knew where that soul would go, and what He said about Judas is just as true for all those who refuse to believe in Him.

E. The Voice in Heaven (14:13)

Next John heard a voice from heaven saying to him, "Blessed are the dead which die in the Lord from henceforth." Then the Holy Spirit confirmed and guaranteed that voice: "Yea,...that they may rest from their labours; and their works do follow them."

Those who belatedly believe in Jesus Christ will all die as martyrs at the hands of the Antichrist. Even the two witnesses die that way. During that time it will be more blessed to take rest before God and be recognized with the merit of martyrdom than to live — only to be cast eventually into the lake burning with fire and brimstone.

F. Two Harvests (14:14-20)

1. *The First Harvest*

Next come two harvests. Verse 14 says a man like the Son of man was sitting on a white cloud with a golden crown on His head and a sharp sickle in His hand, and He was reaping. That One is Jesus Christ. During the second half of the tribulation Jesus will reap the remaining martyrs. From then on, no one will be saved. Later we will see those martyrs being harvested and coming to heaven.

2. *The Second Harvest*

Then the second harvest begins. This is the last judgment, which reaps unbelievers. It is followed by the war of Armageddon, which will be dealt with in detail in a later chapter. You need to know for now, though, that the war of Armageddon is a war between the saints of Jesus Christ and the armies of the earth. When the second three and one-half years begin, the Antichrist and the people in the world know that the saints will descend from the air to destroy them. They have already seen the 144,000 preachers and the two witnesses taken away into heaven alive. The Antichrist, with all the armies of Europe under his command, plus the eastern kings and their armies, will come to Armageddon to fight against Jesus and His hosts. At that time Jesus will tread down the winepress. The number of people killed will be so great that blood will reach up to the bridles of the horses (see v. 20).

We can easily imagine that John must have seen a nuclear war. Hail and rain fell down heavily. Many people were killed — so many, in fact, that their blood, mixed with the rain, was spread over a distance of 1,600 stadia, or about 180 miles.

VI. THE PLAGUES AND THE JUDGMENT (15:1-16:21)

A. The Last Plague (15:1)

> And I saw another sign in heaven, great and
> marvelous, seven angels having the seven last
> plagues; for in them is filled up the wrath of God
> (15:1).

Things prophesied parenthetically in Revelation 14 are
fulfilled exactly in Revelation 15 and 16. These last
plagues appear in the form of the judgment of seven bowls
and are the final judgment.

B. Those Standing Beside the Sea of Glass (15:2-4)

Just before the final judgment starts, John sees a group
of people standing on the sea of glass mingled with fire.
Those are the people gathered in the final harvest by
Jesus. They don't stand *within* the sea but outside it, for
they have come out of that sea. It represents the world
that is now calm; the world that had only a short time
before sustained severe trials. Those people are the martyrs who were naked and starving and who suffered a
miserable death because they did not worship the beast
and his image.

The song those people sing is "the song of Moses the
servant of God, and the song of the Lamb" (v. 3). It's the
same song the Israelites sang when they saw Pharaoh's
army being engulfed by the Red Sea. After their song,
only dreadful judgment remains.

C. The Judgment of Seven Bowls by the Seven Angels (15:5-16:21)

Next, seven angels received seven bowls containing seven plagues and came out of the temple to pour them out. From Revelation 16-18, only grim judgments are seen. The people who are judged here are those left after God reaps every one who can be saved.

1. *The Plague of the First Bowl (16:2)*

The first angel went and poured his bowl on the earth; strong-smelling sores came upon the bodies of those who bore the mark of the beast. Since anyone without that mark could not sell or buy anything, most people had received it. These individuals suffer intolerable pain because of the sores.

A certain skin disease was prevalent just after the liberation of Korea. I had it, too, and applied quicksilver mixed with sulfur all over my body. I still remember the acute pain that made me jump up and down in the room. However, the sores from the plague of the first bowl will be far more painful.

2. *The Second Bowl (16:3)*

The second angel poured out his bowl on the sea, and it became like the blood of a dead man, killing every living thing in the sea. That reminds us of the miracle Moses performed, turning the water of the Nile River into blood according to the command of God (see Exod. 7:20-25).

3. *The Third Bowl (16:4-7)*

The third angel poured his bowl upon the rivers and the fountains of waters, and they also became blood.

Thus, the people had no drinkable water, so they suffered from thirst. Then the angel of the waters praised God: "Thou art righteous, O Lord, which art, and wast, and shalt be, because thou hast judged thus. For they have shed the blood of saints and prophets, and thou hast given them blood to drink; for they are worthy" (vv. 5-6).

Then another voice came out of the altar and responded, "Even so, Lord God Almighty, true and righteous are thy judgments" (v. 7). His judgments really are fair. He is the righteous judge who redresses our grievances.

4. The Fourth Bowl (16:8-9)

The fourth angel poured his bowl upon the sun, and the heat of the sun increased greatly, killing innumerable people. Even now, in a country like India, the sudden assault of brutal heat brings death to many people.

Notice that even though people are scorched to death by that murderous heat, the survivors still do not repent. Their hearts are hardened to the end. Accordingly, they murmur and blaspheme God.

5. The Fifth Bowl (16:10-11)

The fifth bowl was poured upon the throne of the beast, the Antichrist, filling his kingdom with darkness. "To be brightened" stands for hope, but "to be darkened" stands for the decline of the kingdom and its power. As a consequence, chaos arises and the people are panic-stricken. Although they gnash their teeth and bite their tongues due to extreme pain, they still do not repent of their sins. Instead they blaspheme God.

6. The Sixth Bowl (16:12-16)

The sixth angel poured his bowl upon the great
Euphrates River, and its water dried up in order to make
a way for the kings of the East to advance to the west.

As you have read previously, the Orient's (China's)
army of 200 million is watching for an opportunity to
invade the West so it can attack the Antichrist. Then the
kingdom of the Antichrist suddenly begins to decline and
slip into confusion. The political, economic and military
power the Antichrist has exerted is weakened, the balance of power is broken, and the army of the East invades,
having the upper hand.

At that time, "three unclean spirits like frogs come out
of the mouth of the dragon, and out of the mouth of the
beast, and out of the mouth of the false prophet" (v. 13).
They go forth to the kings of the West and their kingdoms
and seduce them to form an alliance against the Oriental
invasion. The allied forces come to a place called Armageddon. The two enormous armies, totaling as many as
300 million soldiers and equipped with ultra-modern
weapons, gather together for a showdown.

Armageddon is the present plain called Megiddo. The
last time I visited Israel, I learned that Armageddon is
very similar to Kim-hae Plain in Korea — both are surrounded by mountains and located at a strategic transportation center. To the north it leads to Syria and Asia;
to the south it leads to Egypt and the rest of Africa.

When a great massacre breaks out on this plain, Jesus
Christ will descend, accompanied by His saints. At that
point, the armies will cease fighting each other and unite
in a struggle against Jesus and His hosts, but they will
finally suffer defeat (see Rev. 19).

Verse 15 gives a clear warning about Jesus' coming to
the battlefield of Armageddon. "I come as a thief. Blessed
is he that watcheth, and keepeth his garments, lest he

walk naked, and they see his shame."

7. *The Seventh Bowl (16:17-21)*

The seventh angel poured his bowl into the air, and a great voice sounded from the throne of heaven, saying, "It is done." Voices, thunderings and lightnings filled the air, and the greatest earthquake in history divided Jerusalem into three parts. High mountains were brought low, and deep valleys were filled. Jerusalem was being made fit to be ruled by Jesus Christ, the King of kings and Lord of lords.

Cities all over the earth are shaken by the earthquake; the configuration of the earth's surface will undergo severe changes, causing calamities everywhere. Among them, the severest judgment will come upon great Babylon. God will completely destroy that wicked city where the Antichrist rules.

VII. THE RELIGION OF THE GREAT WHORE (17:1-18)

The natural calamities end in Revelation 16, and in chapter 17 the religion of the great whore comes under judgment.

During the great tribulation the Antichrist unites the religions of the world into one. Even today the movement to unite Christianity with other religions is briskly underway. The Antichrist will take advantage of this accommodation to consolidate his foundation for the first three and one-half years. At the beginning of the second part of the tribulation, however, he will persecute this religious unity and crush it to pieces. Revelation 17 tells how he sets up his own idol and exterminates other religions.

A. The Judgment of the Great Whore (17:1-2)

In Revelation 17 the judgment of the great whore, signifying religion, begins. The Bible calls corrupted religion spiritual adultery (see James 4:4). And the great whore represents a depraved and corrupt religion that, like an adulterous bride, follows the idol and the devils, turning away from God. This great whore forms a huge religious body. Taking advantage of its vast organization, she not only worships the Antichrist but also uses him. In turn, the Antichrist politically uses the great whore.

This great whore sits upon many waters. As previously explained, water symbolizes the crowd in every nation, tongue and people. The great whore already has her roots in the whole of mankind. The religions that do not serve God, including Islam, Buddhism and Taoism, are the adulteresses.

Verse 2 says this great whore has committed fornication with the kings and inhabitants of the earth. Throughout history, in spite of the modern assertion that politics and religion should be separate, they have actually taken advantage of each other. In Korean history, for instance, throughout the era of the Three Kingdoms and the Koryo dynasty, Buddhism served as the state religion. During the Yi dynasty, Confucianism was the guiding spirit. In European history Christianity has been and continues to be the political prop.

History tells us a wholesome religion enlivens a nation as well as an individual. Unwholesome religion, on the other hand, brings misery to the lives of both individuals and the state by stealing away their hearts from God and corrupting them.

B. A Woman Sitting Upon a Scarlet-colored Beast (17:3-18)

1. The Kingdom of the World

The scarlet beast of verse 3, with its seven heads and ten horns, is the Antichrist. The seven heads represent the seven kingdoms and their kings that continuously oppose God. The ten horns represent the ten countries that will form the union of Europe.

The great whore sits upon the Antichrist during the tribulation. This means she will achieve religious unification by using the Antichrist politically.

2. The Figure of the Great Whore

She is said to be "arrayed in purple and scarlet colour, and decked with gold and precious stones" (v. 4). This signifies her great pomp. The golden cup in her hand is a religious cup full of abominations and the filthiness of her fornication. Those who drink from the cup become full of evil spirits. Upon the forehead of the whore was written, "Mystery, Babylon the Great, the mother of harlots and abominations of the earth" (v. 5). She is called "Babylon the Great" because she is the religion started in Babylon, as we saw in Revelation 2.

Every corrupt religion in the world today has been influenced by the Babylonian religion. Even within Christendom, bodies of the old and new church are trying to form an ecumenical council with other religions — not to mention the Christian denominations violating the orthodox faith of the Bible. In this move toward consensus, all the religions of the world are being gradually united. At the beginning of the tribulation, backed by the power of the Antichrist, union will be achieved quickly. This is the true character of the great whore.

What you must know for certain is that at the end of the world Christendom will be distinctly divided into two groups: one will be the church united politically and institutionally, and the other will be the church united by the Holy Spirit. Churches that genuinely love Jesus will come together, rising above denominations. Christian organizations that follow the trend of modernism and the new theology will be united according to their political concern, advocating social reform.

Denomination has no meaning before God. What matters is whether a church receives the Holy Spirit at its center and surrenders itself to Him.

3. The Behavior of the Woman

This woman is said to be "drunken with the blood of the saints, and with the blood of the martyrs of Jesus" (v. 6). Her corrupt religion, backed by the power of the Antichrist, will be the first to kill those who have been converted by the evangelization of the 144,000 and the testimony of the two witnesses.

4. The Mystery of the Beast

As previously mentioned, the beast of this passage is the Antichrist. It will come out of the bottomless pit. Theologians speculate about him in several ways. However, his identity has not yet been disclosed. One thing is clear: God will one day release him, a spiritual being, out of hell and cause him to be born into this world as a human being, imitating Jesus by putting on flesh.

My belief is that the Antichrist is already in the world. Before long he will emerge and become a conspicuous figure in the political world. Although his appearance on stage is now suppressed by the power of the Holy Spirit, he will be revealed as soon as the church is taken up into heaven.

Verse 9 says the seven heads of the Antichrist are seven mountains. Seven hills always refer to Rome, for Rome was built on seven hills. Hence, some people speculate that Rome will be the headquarters from which the Antichrist will rule the world.

Verse 10 also says that among the seven heads, or kings, "five are fallen, and one is, and the other is not yet come." The five kingdoms — Assyria, Babylon, Egypt, Medo-Persia and Greece — have already fallen. One is, which was Rome — the kingdom existing in the time of John — and the seventh kingdom is yet to come. According to the passage, when this kingdom comes, it will continue for only a brief time. Then the kingdom of the Antichrist will come as the eighth (see v. 11).

The seventh kingdom is the union of the ten European countries that will arise in the former territory of ancient Rome. For the first three and one-half years of the tribulation, united Europe will keep coalition with the Antichrist through compromise. When that period ends, the eighth kingdom, ruled by the Antichrist, will emerge out of the seventh. He will be supported by three of the ten nations, and the remaining seven will be subdued by his autocratic rule.

Verses 12-14 further say that the ten horns are ten kings and that these kings will give their power and strength to the beast. He, in turn, will oppose the Lamb, the King of kings and the Lord of lords, in the Armageddon war but will eventually be destroyed.

The fate of the great whore sitting on the beast is tragic. This religious organization will get along well with the Antichrist, as they take advantage of each other for three and one-half years. As soon as the second half of the tribulation begins, however, the whore is forsaken. The Antichrist will set up his kingdom and deify himself, erecting his own idol and quickly getting rid of her. In this way religious Babylon falls.

VIII. BABYLON THE GREAT (18:1-24)

Revelation 17 shows the downfall of the great whore, religious Babylon. Now Revelation 18 declares the fall of political and economic Babylon. In other words, the Bible shows here the miserable destruction of the Antichrist.

A. The Fall of Babylon the Great (18:1-2a)

Political and economic Babylon, the city where the Antichrist has wielded power for the second half of the tribulation, is now destroyed, not only by an earthquake and judgment, but also by nuclear weapons launched by the army from the East. Those weapons will blow the city to pieces.

Babylon the great is the place that always rejects God. It opposes Him not only spiritually but also politically and economically.

B. The Situation of Babylon the Great (18:2-3)

Verse 2 also says that Babylon the great has become "the habitation of devils, and the hold of every foul spirit, and a cage of every unclean and hateful bird." As the capital of Satan's Antichrist, it attracts all the fallen angels and unclean spirits. They will make it an evil and degenerate city, worse than Sodom and Gomorrah.

Every nation will have betrayed God and kneeled down to Satan; none can survive if it provokes the Antichrist. He will possess unprecedented economic power (see v. 3).

144

C. The Warning of God (18:4-7)

"And I heard another voice from heaven, saying, Come out of her, my people, that ye be not partakers of her sins, and that ye receive not of her plagues" (v. 4). Thus begins a warning of God to His people against being engulfed in the judgment coming to those who partake of the ungodly assembly of politics and business.

D. The Judgment Against Babylon the Great (18:8-24)

The Bible tells in detail the judgment that will come upon Babylon the great: "Therefore shall her plagues come in one day, death, and mourning, and famine; and she shall be utterly burned with fire: for strong is the Lord God who judgeth her" (v. 8).

In a single day the capital of the Antichrist's kingdom will be burned to ashes by a great explosion. Nothing other than nuclear arms can accomplish that. I believe the 200 million-strong army coming from China will pound this capital with nuclear missiles launched from both the air and the earth. Mushroom clouds ascending from the site will be seen far and wide by sailors upon the sea (see vv. 17-19).

Observing the calamity, the other kings who have been on friendly terms with the Antichrist now mourn for him. The merchants who have traded in this capital will also weep and mourn over him (see vv. 9-11).

Holy apostles and prophets in heaven, on the other hand, are told to rejoice over Babylon's destruction, for God has avenged those who were robbed and killed (see v. 20).

"And a mighty angel took up a stone like a great millstone, and cast it into the sea, saying, Thus with violence shall that great city Babylon be thrown down, and shall be found no more at all" (v. 21). The kingdom of the Antichrist is so completely ruined that it will have no strength left to rise again.

So far we've seen judgments that have fallen upon the world of nature and against the Antichrist and corrupt religion and government. In Revelation 19 we will see Jesus Christ holding the marriage supper of the Lamb and then coming down to Armageddon, accompanied by His bride.

IX. JESUS' COMING DOWN TO THE EARTH (19:1-21)

A. Praise in Heaven (19:1-5)

Revelation 19 begins with a great voice of many people in heaven praising God for judging religious and political Babylon, and rejoicing over the political downfall of the Antichrist.

With the second "Alleluia," smoke rose up forever and ever (see v. 3). It is the smoke of judgment. That means God has cast the Antichrist and his followers into the lake burning with fire and brimstone.

Then the twenty-four elders and four living creatures fell down and worshipped God, saying, "Amen; Alleluia." The word "Hallelujah" is frequently used among people who have received the Holy Spirit. If you say it to those who have not received the Holy Spirit, they will be perplexed. To those who have received the Holy Spirit, however, "Hallelujah, Amen!" is our greeting both now and after we go to heaven.

Then a voice came out of the throne saying, "Praise our God, all ye his servants, and ye that fear him, both small and great" (v. 5). Praise is the fruit God has put on our lips. Many people come to me complaining, "I don't know how to pray. I have nothing to pray for. Even though I kneel down to pray all through the night, I don't know what to pray for."

I always give them the same answer: "Why don't you sing praises then?" The sacrifice of praise becomes the prayer of great glory.

B. The Announcement of the Marriage Supper of the Lamb (19:6-8)

Another voice, like the sound of many waters and the voice of mighty thunder, announces that the world that will be ruled by God is at hand. The beautiful time will soon come when all opposition to God is crushed, Satan is put into custody, and the whole universe is brought under the sovereign rule of God. Accepting that through faith, all the saints announce and celebrate the reigning of God.

At the end of the tribulation the marriage supper of the Lamb is held. We have been engaged to Jesus a long time. Even though we haven't actually met our Bridegroom, Jesus has already made us to sit as His bride. And at some day set aside by God, Jesus will come and lead us into the marriage supper.

> For the Lord himself shall descend from heaven with a shout, with the voice of the archangel, and with the trump of God: and the dead in Christ shall rise first: then we which are alive and remain shall be caught up together with them in the clouds to meet the Lord in the air: and so shall we ever be with the Lord (1 Thess. 4:16-17).

After we are taken up into heaven, we will receive our reward. We receive salvation freely by the power of the precious blood Jesus shed for us. However, we receive the white linen clothes of Revelation 19:8 as a reward for our behavior on earth. When crowns are given, some will receive an unwithering crown, others a crown of glory, still others a crown of righteousness and others a crown of life. Some will receive a crown of joy and gladness and decorate themselves with it. This will take place seven years after the rapture, when we join our Bridegroom at the marriage supper.

C. Those Who Are Called to the Marriage Supper (19:9)

Verse 9 says that those who are called to the marriage supper are blessed. And if they're blessed, how much more blessed will be those who have become the bride! Who are those called to the marriage supper? The church is the bride of Jesus Christ. After Jesus was resurrected from death, the Holy Spirit descended and established the church; and the church, sanctified by the blood of Jesus Christ, was taken up into heaven before the tribulation began. Therefore, the church is qualified to be the bride — no one else. All who were not caught up into heaven with the church are those who are called to the marriage supper.

The first group of these are the friends of the Bridegroom. In the Old Testament God called Abraham His friend. John the Baptist was the last of the prophets who came in the spirit of the Old Testament, and he said, "He that hath the bride is the bridegroom: but the friend of the bridegroom, which standeth and heareth him, rejoiceth greatly because of the bridegroom's voice: this my joy therefore is fulfilled" (John 3:29).

The Old Testament saints, therefore, are not the bride, but friends of the Bridegroom.

The next group of guests are those who are saved after the church has been taken up into heaven. These have died as martyrs during the tribulation; after going through the sea of glass mingled with fire, they will attend the marriage supper as the bridesmaids.

D. The Great Excitement of John (19:10)

When John saw this scene, he was so overwhelmed by emotion that he tried to worship the angel who had spoken. Of course, John knew well the commandment that we should worship only God. Nevertheless, he was so excited by the news the angel had brought that he tried to worship him. But the angel restrained him saying, "See thou do it not...worship God."

E. Descending of Jesus to the Earth (19:11-16)

After the marriage supper, the church, which has become the bride of Jesus, accompanies Him when He comes down to the earth.

1. A Man Who Sits Upon a White Horse

John saw heaven open followed by a man riding upon a white horse. This was Jesus Christ. In Revelation 6 the Antichrist imitated the figure of Jesus, but this is the real Christ. He is called "Faithful and True," since He was faithful to God unto death, and all His words are true (see v. 11).

Besides, "in righteousness he doth judge and make war." When Jesus comes down to this earth again, He will wipe out all evil. His eyes will see everything, and since He is the King of kings and Lord of Lords, He will wear many crowns (see v. 12). Further, "he had a name written, that no man knew, but he himself. And he was clothed with a vesture dipped in blood" (vv. 12-13). Since the name is secret, we don't know it. The vesture dipped in blood refers to the same precious blood Jesus shed to save mankind.

2. *The Coming Down of the Heavenly Host*

Verse 14 tells us that "the armies which were in heaven followed him upon white horses, clothed in fine linen, white and clean." These people following the Bridegroom are the bride. When Jesus shouts while coming down from heaven with words like a sharp sword, His enemies will fall as leaves in the autumn. The Lord will also smite all the nations of the Antichrist with a rod of iron and tread the winepress of the fierceness and wrath of almighty God against those who followed the devil in rebellion (see v. 15). This battle of Armageddon becomes the last war of mankind.

F. The War at Armageddon (19:17-21)

Verses 17 and 18 tell about the things that will happen at Armageddon. The army advancing from the East is 200 million strong, and the opposing army of the Antichrist will probably not be less than 100 million. While this battle is being fought, Jesus descends to the earth. The earthly forces quickly stop fighting each other and are allied under the leadership of the Antichrist to resist the heavenly host (see v. 19). However, Jesus will annihilate all the earthly forces. Therefore the angel beckoned the birds of the air to come and eat the flesh of the slain (see vv. 17-18).

At the same time, the false prophet who had lured people to worship the beast will also be taken, along with the Antichrist, and both will be cast into the lake of fire burning with sulfur (see v. 20).

From one end of the earth to the other, when the word

of Jesus Christ goes out of His mouth, those who received the mark of the beast on their forehead or hand will all die. As Ananias and Sapphira died immediately by Peter's pronouncement of judgment against them (see Acts 5:1-11), so shall all those people with the mark of the beast be killed (see v. 21).

Besides the Jews who escape to the desert, only a handful of gentiles will survive. These are people who live outside the domain of the Antichrist. Since they are self-sufficient, like farmers, they will not have needed to receive the mark of the beast. As the rule of the Antichrist will concentrate on Europe, the poor people living on other continents will probably belong to this group. The rich and business-class people, however, will have received the mark for the sake of their businesses. They will be killed.

This handful of gentiles, along with the Jews who survive the tribulation, will enter the millennial kingdom, but there will also be distinction there.

SIX

THE MILLENNIAL KINGDOM AND THE GREAT JUDGMENT

I. THE IMPRISONMENT OF SATAN (20:1-3)

The Antichrist and the false prophet were cast into the lake of fire. The same fate will eventually be given to the old serpent that enticed the world — the dragon called the devil or Satan. First, though, John saw "an angel come down from heaven, having the key of the bottomless pit and a great chain in his hand. And he laid hold on the dragon" (vv. 1-2a). He threw this dragon into the bottomless pit, but Satan is not yet cast into the lake burning with fire, for there is still one more thing

153

left for him to do. He is bound in the pit for one thousand years, but then he is loosed again for a short time.

During this millennium the earth is once again populated with people. They neither commit any sin nor are afflicted with any illness, as they are not tempted by Satan or under his influence. They flourish and fill the face of the whole earth.

Therefore these people who have lived in a world free from the influence of Satan need to decide for themselves whether they will truly love God. To test them, Satan is released from the bottomless pit for a little while. This testing is no worse than what has already been experienced by many of God's saints.

II. THE THRONES OF JUDGMENT AND THE FIRST RESURRECTION (20:4-6)

A. The Thrones of Judgment

John next saw thrones that gave judgment to the people before they entered the millennial kingdom. Why should it be "thrones" instead of "a throne"? Because Jesus does not give judgment alone; His bride, the church, will sit with Him and judge. Hallelujah! This is what is meant by the words, "They...reigned with Christ a thousand years" (v. 4).

How will those thrones give judgment? As we have already seen, the people who were sealed by the Antichrist were all killed, but those who were not sealed by him, and the remaining Jews, will enter the millennial kingdom. Out of those God will separate the sheep from the goats as Jesus said in Matthew 25. The standard by which the two are separated is how they treated Jesus Christ:

When the Son of man shall come in his glory, and

all the holy angels with him, then shall he sit
upon the throne of his glory: and before him shall
be gathered all nations: and he shall separate
them one from another, as a shepherd divideth
his sheep from the goats: and he shall set the
sheep on his right hand, but the goats on the left.
Then shall the King say unto them on his right
hand, Come, ye blessed of my Father, inherit the
kingdom prepared for you from the foundation
of the world: for I was an hungered, and ye gave
me meat: I was thirsty, and ye gave me drink: I
was a stranger, and ye took me in: naked, and ye
clothed me: I was sick, and ye visited me: I was
in prison, and ye came unto me.... Then shall he
say also unto them on the left hand, Depart from
me, ye cursed, into everlasting fire, prepared for
the devil and his angels: for I was an hungered,
and ye gave me no meat: I was thirsty, and ye
gave me no drink: I was a stranger, and ye took
me not in; naked, and ye clothed me not: sick,
and in prison, and ye visited me not (Matt.
25:31-43).

The sheep on the right side of Jesus were the people
who, though they did not believe in Him, nonetheless
treated Christians well by taking care of their needs. The
goats, however, were punished, for they did not accept
Christians in the name of Christ.

B. The First Resurrection

At this first resurrection (see v. 5), those who died
during the tribulation rise first. Those who partake in
this resurrection are blessed, for they will not enter the
second death. The first death is the death of the body, and
the second is the death of the soul, which means that one

is forsaken by God and dies forever.

Those who participate in the first resurrection, however, are received by God and will reign with Christ for one thousand years. How blessed those people will be!

The rest of the dead do not come to life until the thousand years are ended. All the sinners since the beginning of the world will remain in hell; they will not enter the millennial kingdom. After Jesus' reign of one thousand years has ended, those unbelievers will come to life again and be judged. Then they will be cast forever into the lake of fire.

Therefore the resurrection of sinners becomes a resurrection to judgment and destruction. But the resurrection of those who have participated in the first resurrection is a rising to eternal life.

III. SATAN IS LOOSED OUT OF HIS PRISON (20:7-10)

At the conclusion of the millennium, God releases Satan from the bottomless pit. This gives Satan a free hand to go about the world and entice people as he once did. Realizing this is his last chance, he gathers his people to oppose God. "Gog and Magog" refer to the people who oppose God (see v. 8).

Among the people who follow Satan are those who have enjoyed the reign of Jesus and His saints for one thousand years. Nevertheless, when they are exposed to the temptation of the devil, they sympathize with and follow him. They baffle me. Verse 8 says the number of those who follow the devil is like the sand of the sea. Therefore, even out of this group, God will select His people through a test.

As a thief turns on his master with a club, so the people following Satan will come to besiege the holy city of Jerusalem, where Christ and His saints dwell. The world will be sharply divided into two groups: those who are inside the city and those on the outside; wheat and tares; sheep and goats (see v. 9).

God will destroy, like tares, those people who are encamped outside the city, and their souls will fall headlong into the lake of unquenchable fire. Moreover, the evil trinity that deceived them — Satan, the Antichrist and the false prophet — will also fall into the lake of fire, where they will be tormented forever and ever (see v. 10).

On the other hand, those who followed Jesus in the millennial kingdom will enter the eternal new heaven and the new earth.

IV. THE JUDGMENT OF THE GREAT WHITE THRONE (20:11-15)

Then suddenly the heaven and the earth disappear (see v. 11). Will the earth be gone forever? No. Ecclesiastes 1:4 says, "One generation passeth away, and another generation cometh: but the earth abideth for ever." Therefore it's not that the earth has gone forever, but that our Lord is going to transform it. The scene of transforming the earth is recorded in 2 Peter 3:10:

> But the day of the Lord will come as a thief in the night; in the which the heavens shall pass away with a great noise, and the elements shall melt with fervent heat, the earth also and the works that are therein shall be burned up.

Thus, there was found no place for the heaven and the earth, and a throne of judgment is set at a certain place within the universe. This is the white throne, and when the judgment finally begins, all the dead rise and stand before it. Then the books in which are recorded the deeds of every man and woman are opened. There's no hiding at that point.

Verse 12 next says that another book was opened — the book of life. Why is the book of life needed to judge the dead? Because God is righteous, and after He points out every unrighteous behavior of sinners, He opens the book of life and shows them that their names are not recorded. Everyone whose name is not recorded in the book of life falls into the lake of fire without being able to say anything for vindication.

This is the second death — that is, the soul is permanently separated from God and tormented forever. The lake of fire is a place of no hope. Jesus said concerning it, "Where their worm dieth not, and the fire is not quenched. For every one shall be salted with fire, and every sacrifice shall be salted with salt" (Mark 9:48-49).

Those drunken and wanton people who are given to all kinds of filthiness and wickedness today will die like withering grass on the day when they hear the shout and trumpet call of the archangel. Their souls will wait in hell, and after they are judged before the great white throne, they will fall into the lake of fire, where they will be tormented forever.

In the Old Testament the harlot, Rahab, saved the lives of her parents, brothers, sisters and relatives by gathering them at her house and warning them not to go out when Jericho fell at the hands of the Israelites (see Josh. 6:17-25). How much more should we then make our best efforts to save our loved ones! Our efforts must be extended to include our neighbors, as well. The reward for what we have done to save souls will be great, and we shall be happy and joyful in heaven.

SEVEN

THE NEW HEAVEN AND THE NEW EARTH

I. THE NEW HEAVEN AND THE NEW EARTH (21:1)

People always like new things — new food, new clothes, new furniture and new experiences. Whenever they can afford it, they look with eagle eyes for new things.

The heaven we shall enter is new forever. It will be new every morning we wake up, and get newer day by day. The more we see it, the fresher it will look to us. That is why its name is the new heaven and the new earth.

Nobody gets old, nor does anyone grow weak. There is nothing filthy there.

In this world everything gets old, stale and weak. Human beings also grow old and feeble. Everything we use gets stained, soiled and shabby. But the new heaven and the new earth God gives is new forever.

Isn't that our wish and hope? Don't we strive every day to live a good and righteous life since we have received salvation through the precious blood of Jesus Christ? Isn't that what we seek to obtain while fighting the good fight and finishing our course, keeping ourselves from the pleasures and comforts of the world? Praise the Lord! God will grant our wish so richly that there won't be room enough to receive the blessing. God is faithful, and His Word is true. We cannot imagine what the blessed new heaven and new earth will be like. Our hearts will leap with joy, and we will be spellbound by its splendor. We will sing praises of "Hallelujah" forever.

In this new heaven and new earth everyone will retain freshness and youth forever and be in the presence of the Lord. Now the human body inevitably grows old, but not when the new heaven and new earth come into being.

There is no sea in the new heaven and the new earth (see 21:1). Why? We sometimes call life the sea of trouble. The sea stands for bitterness and sorrow. But there is no pain of any kind in the new heaven and the new earth.

II. THE NEW JERUSALEM (21:2-4)

John also saw descending from heaven the new Jerusalem, the capital of the new heaven and the new earth.

Who will live in the new Jerusalem? The church that is the bride of Jesus Christ will enter it with her Bridegroom and live there forever. The Jews and those who are saved during the millennial kingdom will also live in the new heaven and new earth.

The new Jerusalem is so beautiful it is said to be like a bride adorned for her husband (see v. 2). Imagine the beauty of a bride as she appears wearing many precious jewels. In the not-too-distant future we shall enter this amazing city ourselves and live there forever, admiring its beauty. We will worship and praise God forever, and He will wipe away all tears from our eyes, and there will be no more death (see v. 4).

When I was pioneering my ministry at Pulkwang-dong, a couple from Choongchung Province came to live in the community. The husband was a carpenter. They accepted Jesus and began to attend my church. Unfortunately, however, the carpenter fell ill with stomach cancer and eventually died. Upon hearing news of his death, I rushed to his house and found a shocking scene. The small rented room was packed with children who were utterly destitute. In the midst of extreme poverty, the bread earner had died. The wife, holding the body of her dead husband, was wailing, "Why did you go alone, leaving me behind in this world with all these little children? Why?" The children were also weeping.

Suddenly the husband opened his eyes, seized both of his wife's hands as well as my hands, and said, "Dear, why are you crying? Is this our eternal separation? I will go first and wait for you to come, praying there to Jesus that God will keep you and our children. So do your best in taking care of our children and bringing them up well. Then come to the place where I am."

As soon as he finished speaking those words, he died again. His countenance looked so bright, as if he were leaving his wife at the airport for a trip to the United States. It was not long before the wife stopped crying. From that time on her spirit revived, and she was able to exert all her effort to improve her life and take good care of the children. The result was she lived a better life than she had when her husband was alive.

That couple could part without much sorrow because they had hope that they would meet again in the kingdom of God. But to those who do not harbor such a hope, death means the end of everything. However, we who will enter the new Jerusalem will no longer experience death or even sorrow. In that place there will be nothing sad and no more pain, for the former things will pass away, and it will become a completely new world.

III. THE PROCLAMATION OF GOD (21:5-8)

I once heard an extraordinary testimony from Maxine Hurston, the wife of a missionary of our church. She wrote of her experience in a Christian magazine called *The Evangel*. I read her testimony and later even met her. Here is her story:

While kneeling in prayer at the altar of the church one Sunday, Mrs. Hurston was slain in the spirit and given a vision.

Led by an angel, she went upward until she arrived at a place called the new Jerusalem. As she prepared to enter, she saw Jesus standing at a gate made of one great pearl. He stretched forth His hand and welcomed her, saying, "Maxine, welcome." Entering the gate, she first saw Stephen passing beside her. She called to him, "Deacon Stephen! May I ask you a question? I read in the Bible that you died in a heap of stones. Was it painful?"

With a smile on his face, Stephen answered: "When the stones rained thick and fast around me, heaven opened, and Jesus stretched out His hand. When I took that hand, I was in heaven. I didn't feel any pain at all."

After a while, she met David and Peter. Both of them welcomed her. Then a man who was a total stranger greeted her as if she were a close relative. Wondering, she asked who he was.

He answered, "You may not know me. You are not to

stay here. You will soon return to the world below, and when you go back, please talk to my mother who lives there. I am the younger brother of your husband, John Hurston. I died several months after I was born." Because Maxine had never heard about this brother of her husband's, she thought it strange.

Then Jesus showed her many places in heaven, and it was just the same as recorded in the Bible. The glory of God shone so brightly that anyone who saw it was dazzled by the light. The river of the water of life flowed in the midst of the street, and on both sides of the river was the tree of life. Under the tree were benches upon which sat saints who had come there earlier. They were chatting intimately with angels.

Maxine saw the marriage supper of the Lamb prepared in a great hall that was so huge you could not see one end from the other. An angel stood outside the hall looking around. He seemed to be waiting for someone. When she asked him, he said, "I am waiting for the bride, and she will come soon."

As she was led back outside, finishing her tour of heaven, someone called to her, "Maxine! Maxine!" Turning around, she saw Abraham running to her. Taking her by the hand, he pleaded, "Maxine, please don't fail to tell my words to my descendants when you go down. Please tell them to remember that a beautiful place is already prepared here. Tell them that they should by all means come here, not giving in to the temptations of the world. Now go and work hard."

When she awakened several hours later, she found herself in the arms of her sobbing husband. She immediately questioned him: "Dear, you have something you have kept from me. I just returned from a visit to heaven where I met someone who called me the wife of his elder brother. Do you have a younger brother who died as an infant?"

Her husband answered, "I had a younger brother who died only a few months after he was born. I had forgotten about him, but maybe my mother still has one of his pictures."

When she recovered from her illness, Maxine went to her mother-in-law and asked to see the picture. Later she told me she saw similarities to the face she had seen in heaven. That is the experience I heard from Mrs. Hurston, after begging her several times to tell it to me, for she was not the kind of person who would tell such a story to just anyone.

As her testimony affirms, heaven is finished adorning itself and is ready to accept us. The marriage supper is also ready. We don't know at what time or hour the Lord will come. The scriptural heaven John saw was also seen and testified of by many people after him, and the testimonies are always the same.

Therefore the proclamation of God, "Behold, I make all things new," is faithful and true (v. 5). God, who is the Alpha and the Omega, said that those who overcome the world and accept Jesus as Savior shall drink freely from the fountain of the water of life (see v. 6). "But the fearful, and unbelieving, and the abominable, and murderers, and whoremongers, and sorcerers, and idolaters, and all liars, shall have their part in the lake which burneth with fire and brimstone: which is the second death" (v. 8).

IV. THE NEW JERUSALEM, THE BRIDE OF THE LAMB (21:9-22:5)

Our adornment today, the adornment of the bride of Jesus Christ, is the same as the adornment of the new Jerusalem. Therefore the appearance of the new Jerusalem is the same as our appearance spiritually. That is why the Bible calls the new Jerusalem the bride of Jesus Christ:

> And he carried me away in the spirit to a great
> and high mountain, and shewed me that great
> city, the holy Jerusalem, descending out of
> heaven from God, having the glory of God: and
> her light was like unto a stone most precious,
> even like a jasper stone, clear as crystal (vv.
> 10-11).

The green color of the precious jasper stone stands for
divinity and life, the spiritual green pasture that provides
eternal life. Therefore the new Jerusalem is a place full
of infinite divinity, inexhaustible satisfaction and endless
life.

> And [it] had a wall great and high, and had
> twelve gates, and at the gates twelve angels, and
> names written thereon, which are the names of
> the twelve tribes of the children of Israel.... And
> the wall of the city had twelve foundations, and
> in them the names of the twelve apostles of the
> Lamb (vv. 12-14).

That description refers to the twelve tribes of Israel
and the twelve apostles of the New Testament age. Therefore the names here are the names of the twenty-four
elders — in other words, the saints who are saved.

> And he that talked with me had a golden reed to
> measure the city, and the gates thereof, and the
> wall thereof. And the city lieth foursquare, and
> the length is as large as the breadth: and he
> measured the city with the reed, twelve thou-
> sand furlongs. The length and the breadth and
> the height of it are equal (vv. 15-16).

Twelve thousand furlongs are 2,400 kilometers, or

about 1,440 miles. So the length, the breadth and the height of the new Jerusalem are all about 1,440 miles. The architecture of heaven is obviously inscrutable, for by human design that kind of structure would be impossible.

> And he measured the wall thereof, an hundred
> and forty and four cubits, according to the meas-
> ure of man, that is, of the angel (v. 17).

Converted to today's measurements, 144 cubits is about forty meters, or more than 120 feet. Hence, the wall of this heavenly city is very thick. Verse 18 says the wall of the city "was of jasper: and the city was pure gold, like unto clear glass." How splendid it will be! The twelve foundations of the wall are made of all kinds of precious stones, and the twelve gates are twelve pearls; each gate is one big pearl (see vv. 19-21).

There is a reason for the gates of the new Jerusalem being made of pearls. Pearls are produced from oysters in the sea. When sand creeps into the oyster's shell, it injures the body of the oyster. Therefore the oyster produces a secretion with its saliva to cover the intruder, and in the process, over a long period of time, a lustrous pearl is formed.

Likewise, the gates of the new Jerusalem are made of pearls because the people who enter all possess faith like pearls. While they lived in the world, they were not discouraged by the numerous trials that came their way. Rather, they overcame them through prayer. They covered the trials and tribulations by producing perseverance and faith.

The city's being made of pure gold means that all the people who enter it will have a divine nature, throwing away their human nature, and will live forever. Besides divinity, gold stands for a king.

And I saw no temple therein: for the Lord God Almighty and the Lamb are the temple of it. And the city had no need of the sun, neither of the moon, to shine in it: for the glory of God did lighten it, and the Lamb is the light thereof. And the nations of them which are saved shall walk in the light of it: and the kings of the earth do bring their glory and honour into it. And the gates of it shall not be shut at all by day: for there shall be no night there. And they shall bring the glory and honor of the nations into it. And there shall in no wise enter into it any thing that defileth, neither whatsoever worketh abomination, or maketh a lie: but they which are written in the Lamb's book of life (vv. 22-27).

In the Old Testament God was in the holy of holies of the temple. In the new Jerusalem, however, because God is with us, there is no need for the temple. Moreover, because the glory of God shines in it and Jesus is its light, we will need neither the sun nor the moon. Hence, there is no more night. In addition, outside the new Jerusalem, the citizens of flesh who enter the new heaven and the new earth after the millennial kingdom become fruitful and multiply. They will rule over nations, having kings at their head. Those kings will continually come to the new Jerusalem, the capital, to make reports and receive orders. But only those whose names are recorded in the Lamb's book of life are able to enter the city.

And he [the angel] shewed me a pure river of water of life, clear as crystal, proceeding out of the throne of God and of the Lamb (v. 22:1).

Under the thrones of the Lamb of God and the Father flows a river as clear as crystal. It winds through the midst of the streets, and on each side is a tree of life that bears twelve "manner" of fruit. The tree yields its fruit monthly, and each piece of fruit tastes different (22:2). People eat this fruit only for the joy of eating, not to fill their stomachs. In heaven we can live without eating. Many people ask me, "Shall we also eat in heaven?" Now you have the answer.

CONCLUSION

A WORD OF PROPHECY

Verse 7 of Revelation 22 says that he who keeps the sayings of the prophecy of this book is blessed. Therefore you who have read this exposition of John's revelation *have been* blessed. If you put the sayings of this prophecy into your heart and keep them, you will be *more* blessed.

Once again, as in Revelation 19:9, John was so greatly moved in his heart that he fell down at the feet of the angel. The same joy and strong emotion should be in the heart of all who read Revelation. We can shout "Hallelujah!" and be blessed.

169

If you do not have this moving emotion in your heart, pray that you may have a firm faith in the words recorded in Revelation and accept them with an amen. I pray in the name of Jesus that you may have such help from the Holy Spirit.

John's revelation has become an open book to us as the angel desired in verse 10. The sayings of the prophecy have been made known to us, for the time draws near. Our response should be to go and preach, sowing the seed of the gospel.

Now is the age of grace. Therefore be a witness for Christ. Soon your words will sprout, and in time, they will grow into a big tree. You will reap people of faith. The day of Jesus' coming draws near. Before it is too late, witness with all your might.

The following verses show that the coming of the Lord is much closer than we realize:

> Behold, I am coming soon! My reward is with me, and I will give to everyone according to what he has done. I am the Alpha and the Omega, the First and the Last, the Beginning and the End. Blessed are those who wash their robes, that they may have the right to the tree of life and may go through the gates into the city (vv. 12-14, NIV).

Our robes signify life. We must live a life of repentance every day, washed by the precious blood of Jesus Christ. And at whatever time the Lord may come to us, we must be ready to be caught up into the air, saying with the Holy Spirit, "Amen! Hallelujah!" Let us be the blessed people who enter the new Jerusalem, the new heaven and the new earth, where we will serve God forever!

I Jesus have sent mine angel to testify unto you

these things in the churches. I am the root and the offspring of David, and the bright and morning star (v. 16).

Once again we see the word *church* that had disappeared since the third chapter of Revelation. However, at the close of the revelation the Lord said to the church:

And the Spirit and the bride say, Come. And let him that heareth say, Come. And let him that is athirst come. And whosoever will, let him take the water of life freely (v. 17).

The bride is the church that has been taken up into heaven, and the Holy Spirit is the One who initiated it. Thus, this scripture means the Holy Spirit and the church preach the gospel hand in hand. Every church should accept the Holy Spirit, and by His power preach the Word of the Lord.

Lastly, the Lord says that plagues will be added to those who add something to this prophecy of the book of Revelation. Likewise, if anyone takes away from the words of this book, God will take away "his part out of the book of life, and out of the holy city, and from the things which are written in this book" (v. 19). Whatever their motives, people should handle God's Word with great care lest they fall under His curse.

Revelation 22:20 reads: "He which testifieth these things saith, Surely I come quickly. Amen. Even so, come, Lord Jesus."

Witnessing things that would happen to the church during the next two thousand years, and the things that would happen during the tribulation following the rapture of the church, John was in fear and disappointment. But after he saw the glorious new heaven and new earth, he was overwhelmed with joy and looked forward to the coming of the Lord. He prayed, shouting with a loud voice, "Amen. Even so, come, Lord Jesus!"

Let that be our prayer, too. The person who has finished reading this book can shout loudly with me:

"Amen. Even so, come, Lord Jesus!"

Daniel
Paul Y. Cho

'At last! Here's someone who not only understands the book of Daniel but can explain it simply.'

Jamie Buckingham

No other book of the Bible does more to reveal the fact that God is in control of the course of history than the book of Daniel. Today with the rapid realignment of political alliances and the rise of new world powers, every Christian needs to return to God's Word to gain His purpose and perspective.

God used a Jewish boy, captured and brought to serve in the court of the kings of Babylon, to prophesy the rise and fall of every kingdom that has ever ruled the world. Daniel foresaw one last kingdom that has yet to appear. Could the foundation of that kingdom be taking shape today?

Paul Yonggi Cho presents a compelling, chapter-by-chapter exposition of the book of Daniel. This Old Testament book not only contains the prophetic keys to understanding history, but Daniel himself provides a most excellent example for all those who want to serve God with courage and conviction. Cho's commentary and insights reveal how practical and relevant this most ancient book is today.

Catalogue Number YB 9222   £3.25

THE HOMECELL GROUP STUDY GUIDE Volume 1

Paul Y. Cho

From the world's largest church comes this *Homecell Group Study Guide*, as used by the 50,000 cell groups, or home groups, which form the basis of the Yoido Full Gospel Church in Seoul, Korea. Its seven volumes provide a systematic study of the entire contents of the Bible over seven years. Each volume is divided into units and weekly lessons, which present the material in a user-friendly format easily accessible to both home groups and individuals. *Key Scripture verses* and *objectives* for lessons are clearly set out, *leading questions* help to focus on the *message* of the day, *closing questions* draw the material together and each lesson ends with suggestions for the *application* of the message in everyday lives.

Volume One covers the following topics: the Creation, the Fall, God's Promise of Redemption, God as Man in Jesus Christ and the Ministry of Jesus Christ.

Jesus commissioned His disciples to go out and teach all people everything He had told them. As Dr Paul Cho says, 'Teaching is to understand rightly the work of God's Creation, Jesus' crucifixion and the Holy Spirit's continuous working among us . . . this book . . . is like building a house of faith with the Word of God on a firm foundation . . .'

Catalogue Number YB 9338   £4.99

THE HOLY SPIRIT: MY SENIOR PARTNER

Paul Y. Cho

Every morning when I awake I greet the Holy Spirit and invite Him to go with me through the day and take the lead in all my affairs, and He does. I say, 'Good Morning Holy Spirit. Let's work together today and I will be Your vessel.' Every evening before retiring I say again, 'It's been a wonderful day working with You, Holy Spirit.'

Paul Yonggi Cho

You can have the same intimate personal relationship with the Holy Spirit that Paul Yonggi Cho says is at the heart of his effective ministry. Cho sees himself as the junior partner of the Holy Spirit in his daily work of accomplishing the portion of God's plan assigned to him.

* Learn how you can let the Holy Spirit be your senior partner in your daily life.
* Be inspired by Paul Yonggi Cho's personal testimony of his working relationship with the Holy Spirit.
* Learn about the person and work of the Holy Spirit, so that you can let Him guide you more effectively.
* Understand and receive the gifts of the Holy Spirit.

Catalogue Number YB 9312   £2.95

PRAYING WITH JESUS

Paul Y. Cho

Prayer is a dialogue with God in which our attitudes and thoughts are grafted into God's thoughts.

In *Praying With Jesus* the author takes us deep into the teaching of the Lord's Prayer. This is the perfect model for our own prayers but more than that, it shows us how to align our thoughts with God's purposes for the world and for His people.

For prayer to be accomplished our thoughts on God must be right, and this is where the book begins. Dr Cho then takes us phrase by phrase through the rest of the Lord's Prayer. He writes not only with theological insight, but as a pastor who has seen these principles working out in people's lives over the years.

If you want to receive clearer answers to your prayers, if you simply want to draw nearer to God, then try *Praying With Jesus*.

Catalogue Number YB 9165   £2.50